Forgiving from the Heart

Forgiving from the Heart

BY

FATHER FRANCIS A. FRANKOVICH, CC

BIBLE TRANSLATION USED:
NEW REVISED STANDARD VERSION
CATHOLIC EDITION

Companions of the Cross

Companions of the Cross
199 Bayswater Avenue
Ottawa, Ontario K1Y 2G5
****

1949 Cullen Boulevard
Houston, TX 77023

www.companionscross.org

Forgiving from the Heart
by Fr. Francis A. Frankovich, CC

Designed by Jaroz.

Imprimatur:
His Eminence Daniel Cardinal DiNardo, D.D., S.T.L.
Archbishop of Galveston-Houston

Contents

Dedication

This book is dedicated to the Most Sacred Heart of Jesus, the Divine Mercy, who took upon Himself the price of our sins to free us from them and all other forms of evil.

I also dedicate this book to the Immaculate Heart of Mary, the most holy mother of Jesus and our mother, who suffered in union with Him with such love so as to intercede for our deliverance from all forms of evil. Thank you Mary!

And finally, I dedicate this book to us who have been wounded by or have wounded another, intentionally or not. Perhaps we have not forgiven or been forgiven. May we see why and how forgiving enables us to be more alive and truly free.

Forgiveness is an action of love. Forgiveness is God in action within us!

Acknowledgements

I am most grateful for all those who participated in this English version of this book through their comments and critiques. I am especially thankful to Fr. Rick Jaworski, CC, Fr. Mark Goring, CC, Ann Martinez, Jose Mattei, Jan Brown, Francoise Bergeron....

Also I thank Jennifer Benitez and Rosa Serrano for all the typing that they did.

Forgiving from the Heart
PREFACE

"Then Peter came and said to him, 'Lord, if another member of the church sins against me, how often should I forgive? As many as seven times?' Jesus said to him, 'Not seven times, but; I tell you, seventy-seven times. For this reason the kingdom of heaven may be compared to a king who wished to settle accounts with his slaves. When he began the reckoning, one who owed him ten thousand talents was brought to him; and, as he could not pay, his lord ordered him to be sold, together with his wife and children and all his possessions, and payment to be made. So the slave fell on his knees before him, saying, 'Have patience with me, and I will pay you everything.' And out of pity for him, the lord of that slave released him and forgave him the debt. But that same slave, as he went out came upon one of his fellow-slaves who owed him a hundred denarii; and seizing him by the throat, he said, 'Pay what you owe.' Then his fellow-slave fell down and pleaded with him, 'Have patience with me, and I will pay you.' But he refused; then he went and threw him into prison until he should pay the debt. When his fellow-slaves saw what had happened, they were greatly distressed, and they went and reported to their lord all that had taken place. Then his lord summoned him and said to him, 'You wicked slave! I forgave you all that debt because you pleaded with me. Should you not have had mercy on your fellow-slave, as I had mercy on you?' And in anger his lord handed him over to be tortured until he should pay his entire debt. So my heavenly Father will also do to every one of you, if you do not forgive your brother or sister from your heart." Matthew 18: 21-35.

In this book I propose that the most freeing, most life-giving, and most profound response to each and every one of life's difficulties is to forgive. I am convinced forgiveness is essential for the total physical and spiritual wellbeing of the person offended and the offender.

Even though there are many books and manuscripts written on the importance of forgiveness, you may still have no idea as to what forgiveness is and how it works. In this small book, I will share with you what effective forgiveness is and how, through being forgiven and forgiving you may have a more abundant life.

Let's consider some of the times when I, and perhaps you too, have experienced pain to the point of feeling overwhelmed by a difficult situation that has taken away your peace. For example: have you ever felt so upset you do not want to forgive the person who hurt you, or you just don't know how? Have you ever committed a wrong you wish you could forget or erase? Have you been hurt, betrayed, or damaged by the actions of another? Have you ever felt sad as if God does not hear you or worse, have you felt hurt that He has permitted something bad to happen to you and/or has done something to harm you? Have you believed it is impossible to be forgiven or to forgive?

If so, this book is for you. In this book I will explore three types of what many call forgiving:

1) Forgiving God: after something terrible has happened to you, you might believe that God must not care. And perhaps you have been told you need to forgive Him.

2) Forgiving yourself: you are so upset by what you have done that you don't know how to react. Even after having asked for forgiveness, you still hang on to that feeling of guilt to which some may say you need to forgive yourself.

3) Forgiving others: your frustration and anger with a situation or what someone has done to you seems so great that you think you cannot or do not want to forgive. You have heard you must forgive from the heart, but you do not know how to do this.

This book is not meant to be a book on the theology of forgiveness. Instead, the intent of this book is to help you understand better the process of forgiveness and how to apply it in a practical way so as to attain inner freedom and peace: the abundant life that Jesus Christ offers us.

As a Catholic priest I have the privilege of having people confide in me about some of the most difficult situations in their lives. For many years I have heard the confessions of people who:

1. Think God is against them specially when He has allowed something or someone to harm them.

2. Seek to be forgiven for their wrongs but are struggling to experience forgiveness.

3. Feel pain and resentment against others who have wronged them or have brushed aside what was done against them.

Because of such situations as these three, I have experienced a great motivation to write this book, to share what I sense the Lord desires for His sons/daughters in these situations so as to obtain the life He is offering us.

Many say that to forgive is one of the most difficult steps to take. Yet, not to forgive hinders one from developing: physically, socially, spiritually and affectively. Many are conscious of the damage anger can cause but not of the benefits that can be derived from forgiveness. Nevertheless, it is often thought to be difficult to achieve forgiveness from the heart so as to obtain the life Jesus offers us.

Among other things this book provides a seven step process of forgiveness for the offenses from people and other hurtful situations. This is a way to truly regain peace and experience the freedom allowing for a fuller and more abundant life.

I will use a dialogue with fictional characters, Tom and Margarita. They are a combination of many people in different situations and relate to every walk of life. I will share with you through these two individuals and their circumstances some of the important principles where forgiveness, when properly understood and utilized, will set you free to experience being more fully alive.

15

When we speak about forgiving from the heart, we often think in terms of feelings and emotions. Feelings or emotions are neither good nor bad in themselves. They come from situations and/or inner thoughts which produce some kind of response which is either good or evil. We can think of these inner reactions like temptations which are not sins, but may result in a negative response (sin), as in the case of an angry feeling becoming resentment, hatred or rage when held within or expressed incorrectly. A life-giving response to the same feeling or emotion of anger would be to forgive this person or situation.

How do you know when you need to forgive?

Feelings are generally useful indicators to help us know when forgiveness is needed. Feelings of irritation, annoyance, frustration, disappointment, anger, can be destructive and even develop into resentments or even hatred, especially when forgiveness does not take place. If these feelings are held within, they can lead to the development of a psychosomatic or even a serious physical illness. When these feelings are expressed by yelling, cursing, gossiping, complaining, and even rage they can become harmful to the other person and also to oneself, the one offended.

Throughout this book I will speak often of the importance of forgiving "the offense and even the irritation." To forgive from the heart requires us to be conscious as to when it is necessary to forgive, whether it is for an offense or merely an irritation.

At times we do not want to deal with the emotions that an offense has created within. We then try to ignore the offense all together. On other occasions, with the passage of time it seems the offense has been forgotten. There are also times when the one who offended us has changed, and so we no longer feel the negative emotions of the offense and therefore we do not see a need to forgive. In all these cases, I would say that it is still very helpful to apply the seven step process of forgiveness so as to attain the conviction that the offense has been released to Jesus and is not remaining within.

I read this comment and translated it from Spanish. I'm not sure who is the author, but it speaks about forgiveness confirming what I want to communicate in this book:

"A perfect family does not exist. We don't have perfect parents, we are not perfect, we don't get married with a perfect person, and we don't have perfect sons and daughters. We have complaints against one another. We disappoint each other. Therefore, a healthy marriage and healthy family does not exist without the practice of forgiveness.

Forgiveness is vital to our emotional health and spiritual survival. Without forgiveness, the family becomes a theater of conflicts and a bastion of grievances. Without forgiveness, the family is sick.

Forgiveness is the sterilization of the soul, the cleansing of the mind, and the liberation of the heart. One who does not forgive has neither peace of mind nor communion with God. The hurt is a poison that intoxicates and kills. Keeping a wound in the heart is a self-destructive gesture...

One who does not forgive becomes sick physically, emotionally, and spiritually. That is why the family must be a place of life and not of death; territory of healing not of disease; a place of forgiveness not of guilt. Forgiveness brings joy where there was sorrow due to a hurt; and healing, where the hurt has caused disease."

(I found this comment on August 12, 2015 on Diario Contraste under the section "Mundo." They say that the comment belongs to Pope Francis, but there is not an official document that proves it.)

Now I will delve with you into a practical way to practice forgiveness from the heart. Because the action to forgive is a command given to us by Jesus, it cannot take place without His assistance (His grace). I ask you to call on the presence of the Holy Spirit to enlighten and empower you to look at your life situations in a new light while reading this book. His presence will assist you in understanding this process and in empowering you to achieve what you may have thought was impossible.

My prayer is that this small book, through the working of the Holy Spirit and Mary's powerful intercession, will be of great help to you in understanding more fully what forgiveness is and in enabling you to practice forgiveness from the heart.

Note: In this book any bold or underlined words or bracketed comments within a quote are my addition.

CHAPTER 1
Forgiving God?

Tom is a successful businessman, who in the eyes of the world would seem to have all any man could long for. But under the facade of worldly success he lives a life bound up with guilt due to his past actions. He carries the wounds of a difficult past. He was raised without a father and only by a mother who had many personal and financial problems. Early on, he found his way to the streets where he began living a life of selfishness and deceit. He learned quickly to cheat and mistreat everyone around him, including himself. He was an angry youth who grew to be an angry man. He did things he cannot even bear to remember. He caused great damage to those around him and even landed in jail for a short time. There, surrounded by his and others' grief over past mistakes, he heard that God forgives but found it difficult to believe fully in this forgiveness. Years have passed, he has a successful business, a wonderful wife and children and many blessings, but he still carries the guilt of his past. He cannot forgive himself or even see how God can love and forgive him completely. Recently, he has begun to question where God was when he felt so abandoned and when he needed Him most.

Margarita has been married to a man who is verbally aggressive and highly demanding. He addresses her with vulgar remarks and pressures her to do more than she can do. Her response has been filled with exasperating anger and frustration. She has let him know that he is unfair, his demands are unrealistic, and has asked him to change. She is fearful because she thinks he does not love her anymore. She even suspects he might be involved in relationships with other women. Margarita has two young children, and so the thought of leaving him scares her and goes against what she expected her life to be. She wants her sons to have a father figure even though he is rarely available to them and when he is, he is harsh and unloving. And she also thinks that they would not survive without him financially. She knows deep down that she is still in love with the man she married even though he has changed for the worse. She prays daily for her marriage.

I suggested to Margarita to go to a marriage counselor, but she said that he would not do it. He has even criticized her for suggesting such a thing; besides their finances are very scarce. She has concluded that the only thing to do is to continue working while waiting with the hope that one day he will change.

Like Tom and Margarita: do you feel distraught because you think no one can forgive you for what you have done? And/or do you live in a difficult situation with people who annoy, oppress and mistreat you? Have you lost your peace because of the anger or resentment you feel about your seemingly hopeless situation? In the midst of such a situation have you ever felt abandoned by God?

Tom and Margarita, in their particular situations, are carrying heavy burdens. They feel abandoned, and they both think God is not helping them. Tom has asked the Lord to free him from his feelings of guilt, but to no avail. At times, they even seem to get worse. Margarita feels abandoned by God who seems to have permitted too many bad things to happen in her life, especially after having asked Him, over and over again for her husband's conversion.

Before we can deal with forgiving self and others, let us look first at what is often called the need to forgive God. Let us ask: is this really what is needed?

The dictionary tells us that to forgive is to cease to feel resentment against the offender; to let go of the emotion or wrong that we experience; or to cancel a debt. With this understanding of forgiveness, let us apply this definition to what is often referred to as "forgiving God."

To do so let us begin by seeing 1) what evil really is. Then we will look at 2) where it comes from. Following this we will look at 3) how God actually provides for us in the event of an evil. Then we will end with 4) what God desires us to do when we get angry with Him because of this evil - what some have called "forgiving God".

1) What is evil?

The following event, which I received by email from a friend, will help us better understand what evil is. It occurred in a university classroom and was initiated by an atheistic professor addressing his students.

The professor, at this well-known institution of higher learning, challenged his students with this question. "Did God create everything that exists?"

A student bravely replied, "Yes he did!"

"God created everything?" The professor repeated. "Yes sir, he certainly did," the student replied. The professor answered, "If God created everything; then God created evil. And, since evil exists, and according to the principle that our works define who we are, then we can assume God is evil."

The student became quiet and did not know how to respond to the professor's hypothetical definition; though he knew the professor was incorrect. The professor, quite pleased with himself, boasted to the students now he had proven once more that religious faith was a myth.

Another student raised his hand and said, "May I ask you a question, professor?" "Of course," replied the professor.

The student stood up and asked, "Professor, does cold exist?" "What kind of question is this? Of course it exists. Have you never been cold?" The other students snickered at the young man's question. He replied, "In fact sir, cold does not exist. According to the laws of physics, what we consider cold is in reality the absence of heat. Every body or object is susceptible to study when it has or transmits energy, and heat is what makes a body or matter have or transmit energy. Absolute zero (-460°F) is the total absence of heat, and all matter becomes inert and incapable of reaction at that temperature. Cold does not exist. We have created this word to describe how we feel if we have no heat."

The student continued, "Professor, does darkness exist?" The professor responded, "Of course it does." The student replied, "Once again you are wrong sir, darkness does not exist either. Darkness is in reality the absence of light. Light we can study, but not darkness. In fact, we can use Newton's prism to break white light into many colors and study the various wave lengths of each color. You cannot measure darkness. A simple ray of light can break into a world of darkness and illuminate it. How can you know how dark a certain space is? You measure the amount of light present. Is this not correct? Darkness is a term used by man to describe what happens when there is no light present."

Finally the young man asked the professor, "Sir, does evil exist?" Now uncertain, the professor responded, "Of course, as I have already said. We see it every day. It is in the daily examples of man's inhumanity to man. It is in the multitude of crimes and violence everywhere in the world. These manifestations are nothing else but evil." To this the student replied, "Evil does not exist, sir, or at least it does not exist unto itself. Evil is simply the absence of God. It is just like darkness and cold, a word that man has created to describe the absence of God. God did not create evil. Evil is the result of what happens when man does not have God's love present in his heart. It's like the cold that comes when there is no heat, or the darkness that comes when there is no light."

The professor sat down.

What this student, Albert Einstein, is pointing out is that evil does not exist, but it is the lack of God that exists. We call it "evil". Therefore, it is not God acting when some evil happens because evil is actually the absence of God (the good). God is and can only do good. God is goodness itself.

2) Where does evil or this lack of God come from?

When God made us, He made us like Himself (Genesis 1:26) with a mind and free will. We are affected by evil, which has in us a threefold origin: the world in the sense that it can model values that create a lack of God; the flesh, that is, our own weakened condition due to original sin even after original sin has been removed through Baptism; and thirdly the devil, who is the "father of lies." We, however, also have free will which enables us to choose the good – God, or evil – the lack of God. When we choose evil, it deprives us of life. Deuteronomy 30:15-18 says, *"See, I have set before you today life and prosperity, death and adversity. If you obey the commandments of the LORD your God that I am commanding you today, by loving the LORD your God, walking in his ways, and observing his commandments, decrees and ordinances, then you shall live and become numerous, and the LORD your God will bless you in the land that you are entering to possess. But if your heart turns away and you do not hear, but are led astray to bow down to other gods and serve them, I declare to you today that you shall perish; you shall not live long in the land that you are crossing the Jordan to enter and possess."*

The Lord reminds us that because of our free will, we can choose the good or the lack of good, evil. From this blessings or curses will occur. He indicates to us that He will not take away our free will. When it seems God is against us, it would help to stop and realize that the disorder and disharmony are not from God but from our choices coming from the sources of evil: the world, the flesh and the devil. He allows evil, in the sense that He gives us the freedom to choose the good or to reject it.

James 1:13-15 explains the origin of sin which is fruit of our choices when facing temptations: *"No one, when tempted, should say, 'I am being tempted by God • for God cannot be tempted by evil and he himself tempts no one. But one is tempted by one's own desire, being lured and enticed by it; then, when that desire has conceived, it gives birth to sin, and that sin, when it is fully grown, gives birth to death."*

3) What does God provide for us when something evil happens?

Because God lacks nothing, He can only be and do what is good. He cannot directly cause an absence of good. Evil results from us, as human beings under the influence of the above three sources of evil, when we choose the absence of God. God allows us to make the choice.

However, God promises to be a merciful God as in Romans 8: 28 *"We know that all things work together for good for those who love God, who are called according to his purpose."* Thus anything bad that happens to us because of our choices and those of others He will turn to good, when we return to Him and entrust the situation into His hands. He wants us to believe His word. *"Heaven and earth will pass away, but my words will not pass away."* (Matthew 24:35). His word and promises are constant and firm. God sent His Son to give us the necessary grace to be victorious over our condition weakened by the world, the flesh and the devil. John 3:16-17 reminds us of this truth: *"For God so loved the world that he gave his only Son, so that everyone who believes in him may not perish but may have eternal life. Indeed, God did not send the Son into the world to condemn the world, but in order that the world might be saved through him."* Jesus declares another truth of supreme importance regarding evil, the lack of God. He tells us that we need to seek His help, His grace, so that He may bring good out of evil (and its impact on us) when He says in John 15:5, *"...Those who abide in me and I in them bear much fruit, because apart from me you can do nothing."*

To illustrate this importance of God changing evil, whose source is the world, the flesh and the devil, into good, let us look at this story, which I received by email from another friend: A man went to a barbershop to have his hair cut and his beard trimmed. As the barber worked, they began to converse and talk about many varied subjects. At one point in the conversation the barber said: "I don't believe that God exists." "Why do you say that?" Asked the customer. "Well, you just have to go out in the street to realize that God doesn't exist. Tell me, if God existed, would there be so many sick people? Would there be abandoned children? If God existed, there would be neither suffering nor pain. I can't imagine a loving God who would allow all of these things." The customer thought for a moment, but didn't respond because he didn't want to start an argument. The barber finished his job and the customer left. As he stepped out of the barbershop, he saw a man with long, stringy, dirty hair and an untrimmed beard. The customer turned back and entered the barber shop again and he said to the barber: "You know what? Barbers do not exist." "How can you say that?" Asked the surprised barber. "I am here, and I am a barber. And I just worked on you!" "No!" The customer exclaimed. "Barbers don't exist because if they did, there would be no people with dirty long hair and untrimmed beards like that man outside. "Ah, but barbers DO exist! That's what happens when people do not come to me." "Exactly!" Affirmed the customer. "That's the point! God too DOES exist! Because people do not look to God for help explains why there is so much pain and suffering in the world."

We want to keep remembering that God sent His Son not to condemn us but to rescue us from all evil. We notice this in a special way in 2 Corinthians 5:21: *"For our sake he made him to be sin who knew no sin so that in him we might become the righteousness of God."*

4) What God desires us to do when we get angry with Him because of some evil.

To forgive God, as some people call it, means for one to come to a true understanding of who God is and what He is about; then, to trust that He always works for the greater good, no matter how things seem to be going. He wants us to know He is with us to lead us through the evils which we, who are under the influence of the sources of evil, have done. He is a merciful God. He asks us to seek Him and trust Him to be good. In other words, God does not promise that we will fully understand why the evil happened, but He does promise to accompany us through the pains of evil, which are the lack of God, as He works good out of evil. 1 John 1:9 states, *"If we confess our sins, he who is faithful and just will forgive us our sins and purify us from all unrighteousness."* *"Purify"* in this passage implies He will, with our repentance, transform what we have altered by our sins.

Therefore God, being wholly good, promises to turn our incorrect choices to good when we entrust them to Him. Therefore, we do not need to forgive God when we feel anger toward Him for what is experienced as evil. Instead, we need to repent from our thinking that He was the source of the evil or by permitting it, He did not know what He was doing or cannot use it for our benefit. We should also renounce the lie that God is not in control or working for us. He wants us to trust that He will turn all into good. What He desires is that we trust Him and surrender to Him the evil which we have experienced.

In Jeremiah 15: 10, 17-21, we find a clear example of the need to repent of our improper understanding of God when something evil happens to us. Here the prophet was upset with God because he was perceiving God as at the source of all of his woes. *"Woe is me, my mother, that you ever bore me, a man of strife and contention to the whole land! I have not lent, nor have I borrowed, yet all of them curse me. I did not sit in the company of merrymakers, nor did I rejoice; under the weight of your hand I sat alone, for you had filled me with indignation. Why is my pain unceasing, my wound incurable, refusing to be healed? Truly, you are to me like a deceitful brook, like waters that fail."* Jeremiah was quite upset with the Lord for the evils He was permitting.

"To this the Lord replied, 'If you turn back, I will take you back, and you shall stand before me. If you utter what is precious, and not what is worthless, you shall serve as my mouth. It is they who will turn to you, not you who will turn to them. And I will make you to this people a fortified wall of bronze; they will fight against you, but they shall not prevail over you, for I am with you to save you and deliver you,' says the LORD. 'I will deliver you out of the hand of the wicked, and redeem you from the grasp of the ruthless.'"

The Lord listened to Jeremiah, but He needed to correct him because Jeremiah did not have a clear understanding as to who God was and what He was planning to do. God cannot do evil because it would mean that He, being God, would be incomplete. He is present only to work good even when He permits evil. God did not empathize with Jeremiah. Instead He asked him to repent and hold a clearer image of who He actually is and what He will do with evil when given to Him. He permitted Jeremiah to experience evil so that He could continue His work through him in an even more powerful way.

I explained to both Tom and Margarita that they needed to go to Him, to repent of the way they perceived Him as if He were the cause of that evil or permitting it for an evil purpose. God only permits evil so as to allow a greater good. They also needed, in the name of Jesus, to renounce their lies about who He is and what He was doing in allowing the evil experiences in their lives and to ask the Holy Spirit to heal them of the irritation they were carrying toward the Lord. This healing would enable Him to help them in each of their given situations. If they continued to think that God was against them and not present to help them, they would have difficulty dealing with forgiveness of self and/or forgiving others. They would be even unable to receive the greater victory over their sins and the offenses and irritations from others that God desired for them.

Here is the prayer I recommended they pray:
Lord Jesus, how merciful and wonderful You are. You are love itself. I realize now that I was making You a scapegoat for all that I and others did wrong, under the influence of the evil one, the devil. I was treating You as if You were at fault by allowing the evils to have happened to me. I renounce in the name of Jesus this lie, and I ask Your forgiveness. Take me into Your arms and wash me clean and give me a new spirit of trust in You, that You are working for my good in all that has been happening to me. Heal the way I reacted against You. Thank You for Your love. I rest now in Your great mercy. Amen. [Pause to receive this newness.]

Afterwards, I asked them to spend some time in quiet awareness of His great love for them and His plan to turn all that had occurred into something very powerfully good as they trusted in Him, loved Him. (Cf. Romans 8: 28.) Upon reflection they might be already seeing the good that He had done.

As they thanked Him and gazed on a crucifix where the victory had been won, they both received a great peace which brought them a deep conviction as to how wonderful God was even in those events of evil, the lack of God. This was a more effective way to handle their angry feelings toward the Lord.

CHAPTER 2
Forgiving Self?

Tom is a quiet man. He had not been attending our parish for a very long time, and today was his second visit with me. He stopped by my office and asked if he might have a word with me. I could see the concern in his eyes. It was clear he needed assistance with something, so I asked him to come in.

Tom: Father, I am a Catholic by birth, though I must admit I have not been to church since I was a small child and I don't really remember much about it. Please forgive me if I say some things that don't sound right. I just thought that, well, I should speak to someone because I have not been feeling right about some things.

Father: Tom, I would be happy to listen to what you are feeling.

Tom: Well, you see, I have had a pretty tough past and now, although things in my life seem good externally, I still feel this pain of guilt inside me for the wrongs I have done. Even though I have brought them to Confession, I just can't seem to let them go.

Father: Can you tell me more about this pain, Tom?

Tom: I think I am afraid of dying without having my sins forgiven for all the awful things I have done. I mean I know I cannot pay the price for what I have done. I have tried to repair what I could. I heard in homilies where the priest says God forgives, but I guess I just don't think He can forgive me. Well, I guess, I mean I just don't deserve it, and I feel this horrible pain about it. What can I do? I see more clearly now after your explanation about forgiving God that He is not against me. Your last prayer with Margarita and myself helped me. But I continue to believe there is something more that I need to do to get free of this guilt. Can you help me?

29

Father: Tom, have you heard of St. Faustina? She was a young sister who eventually became a saint. She lived her life as a sacrifice for others, in imitation of Christ's life.

She offered her personal sufferings in union with Christ to atone for the sins of others. She became an instrument of divine mercy, bringing joy and peace to others. She wrote about what the Lord asked her to do in order to encourage others to trust in Him and in His Mercy.

I will share a quote from her Diary #1485. St. Faustina experienced this dialogue between a sinful soul and Jesus:

*"**Jesus:** Be not afraid of your Savior, O sinful soul. I make the first move to come to you, for I know that by yourself you are unable to lift yourself to me. Child, do not run away from your Father; be willing to talk openly with your God of mercy who wants to speak words of pardon and lavish His graces on you. How dear your soul is to Me! I have inscribed your name upon My hand; you are engraved as a deep wound in My Heart.*

***Soul:** Lord, I hear your voice calling me to turn back from the path of sin, but I have neither the strength nor the courage to do so.*

***Jesus:** I am your strength; I will help you in the struggle.*

***Soul:** Lord, I recognize Your holiness, and I fear You.*

***Jesus:** My child, do you fear the God of mercy? My holiness does not prevent Me from being merciful. Behold, for you I have established a throne of mercy on earth - the tabernacle - and from this throne I desire to enter into your heart. I am not surrounded by a retinue or guards. You can come to Me at any moment, at any time; I want to speak to you and desire to grant you grace.*

***Soul:** Lord, I doubt that You will pardon my numerous sins; my misery fills me with fright.*

***Jesus:** My mercy is greater than your sins and those of the entire world. Who can measure the extent of My goodness? For you I descended from* *heaven to earth; for you I allowed Myself to be nailed to the cross; for you I let my Sacred Heart be pierced with a lance, thus opening wide the source of mercy for you. Come, then, with trust to draw graces from this fountain. I never reject a contrite heart. Your misery has disappeared in the depths of My mercy. Do not argue with Me about your wretchedness. You will give Me pleasure if you hand over to me all your troubles and grief. I shall heap upon you the treasure of My grace.*

Soul: *You have conquered, O Lord, my stony heart with Your goodness. In trust and humility I approach the tribunal of Your mercy, where You Yourself absolve me by the hand of Your representative. O Lord, I feel Your grace and Your peace filling my poor soul. I feel overwhelmed by Your mercy, O Lord. You forgive me, which is more than I dared to hope for or could imagine. Your goodness surpasses all my desire. And now, filled with gratitude for so many graces, I invite You into my heart. I wandered, like a prodigal child gone astray; but You did not cease to be my Father. Increase Your mercy toward me, for You see how weak I am.*

Jesus: *Child, speak no more of your misery; it is already forgotten. Listen, My child, to what I desire to tell you. Come close to My wounds and draw from the fountain of life whatever your heart desires. Drink copiously from the Fountain of life and you will not be weary on your journey. Look at the splendors of My mercy and do not fear the enemies of your salvation. Glorify My mercy."*

Father: From this dialogue, Tom, you can see how delighted the Lord is in forgiving you. This is especially granted in the Sacrament of Reconciliation.

When Jesus died on the cross, He paid the price to free us from two basic sins that weigh upon us: mine and theirs, as well as death, the consequence of sin. Jesus taught us this in the prayer of the "Our Father": *"forgive us our trespasses as we forgive those who trespass against us."* Forgiving others also requires an awareness of the forgiveness of the Lord for my sins.

Tom, there are times when having repented of my sins and having confessed them, I too still feel guilty for some things I did in the past. It hangs on to me. I realize the Lord Jesus did not pay the price on the Cross for me to continue to wallow in my sins. He came to free me when I repent, with a contrite heart, and use His wisdom and strength to amend my life.

Tom: What can be done when the guilt of what I did does not leave me?

Father: I can remember a time when I was very unkind to a certain person, in the way I spoke to him and treated him over a period of a week. When I looked back on it, I felt a lot of guilt. I could not believe I acted the way I did. I asked the Lord for forgiveness with as contrite a heart as I could and with a desire to amend my life, but I still felt so bad for what I had done.

Here are some steps I sensed the Lord wanted me to take to overcome this. I asked the Lord for forgiveness and brought it to the Sacrament of Reconciliation. I became aware I needed also to receive forgiveness in the Sacrament and be firm in holding on to the conviction that it was forgiven and healed. I sensed the Lord reminding me: "Did I not pay the price for your sin when I died on the cross? Has not the price been paid? Was this not sufficient to free you from your sin?" Then I sensed He wanted me to hold a crucifix in my hands and gaze on it until He moved deeply within me to convince me I had been washed clean. As I did this, I became aware of 1John1:9 where St. John says: "If we confess our sins, he who is faithful and just will forgive us our sins and cleanse us from all unrighteousness." Jesus was reminding me He not only took the sin away, but that he was also cleansing me. He was doing something good out of my evil behavior, which for me felt so disgusting. As I kept gazing on the crucifix, I imagined myself holding filthy and smelly, worse than sulfur, mud in my hand. Then, as I cried to the Lord to be free of this, I saw Him coming, taking the mud and washing me clean. He took the mud, dried it, perfumed it and made it into a vase that He painted and glazed. He came to me and gave me the vase. I asked Him what this was, and He said it was my sins of which I had repented. I looked at the vase and smelled it and said: "These cannot be my sins." Then He said it was my sins after I repented. He forgave them, took them away, and purified them.

Then He also gave me the image of the prodigal son returning home, (Luke 15). The father ran toward his returning son and kissed him, put a ring on his finger, sandals on his feet, and a new robe around him. Then with delight at his return, he called the servants to kill the fattened calf and ordered a celebration to begin because his son had returned. I sensed Him treating me as the "Prodigal Son."

As all this came upon me while I gazed on the crucifix, I rejoiced in what the Lord was doing in me and even in the one I had offended, although I did not deserve His mercy.

From this experience I sensed that I received the grace to see my sin, to repent of it with a contrite heart and a firm purpose of amendment, and also to spend time receiving directly from the Lord His forgiveness and the good He was doing despite the evil I had done. This is what I considered "forgiving myself."

Often some sins do not seem to weigh so heavily as others. Yet even in these situations, it is important to ask for forgiveness from Jesus and to receive in some concrete way His forgiveness and His wisdom so as to walk in a new way specially through the grace of the Sacrament of Reconciliation. With this, one is healed for what he/she has done because of His great mercy.

Without this sense of forgiveness, it is very difficult to be willing or to want to forgive another. I will speak about this latter element in the third step when I speak about forgiving others, where I will focus on being aware of God's mercy so that you may be able to show God's mercy to the one(s) who offended you or those who merely irritated you.

Tom: Please, Father, pray with me right now so I can receive His forgiveness for all I have done and have already brought to the Sacrament of Reconciliation. I need the Holy Spirit to free me from all this guilt.

Father: Pray along with me: **Lord Jesus, thank You for the great mercy that You have for sinners. I deserve only punishment for all of my sins. I am sorry for having offended You, myself, and others.** [Visualize, as we pause here, Jesus on the cross; look at all His suffering; hear Him remind you: I have endured all this pain, suffering and rejection in order to pay for your sins so that you may be freed from them. Now say] **Thank**

You, Lord Jesus for paying for my sins so that I could be set free. I receive in faith Your forgiveness for all that I have done. Please also forgive the way that I have held on to the guilt even after I had confessed my sins with a contrite heart and with the plan to change my life with your grace. [Spend some time quietly thanking Jesus for the victory over all these sins. Then take a moment to plan a few acts of penance in order to make reparations for the sins you committed. Rejoice that you are free whether you feel it or not. Jesus is faithful and true. He came to set you free and not to condemn you. Let Mary take you under the mantle of her protection so you can continue to walk in this new freedom and life Jesus is giving you].

Tom: Thank you. I sense a deep peace. Even more, I am thoroughly convinced Jesus has taken away my sins and is transforming my evils into something good. Like never before, I am aware of how merciful God really is.

Father: If it is possible, reconcile with some of the people you have hurt. Tell them what you did wrongly and that you are sorry. Ask them to forgive you. This will also help. Ask the Lord to present the opportunity to ask for forgiveness for what you mentioned as having done improperly. If they don't forgive you, God still has forgiven you as you have repented; God's decision to forgive is not dependent upon theirs.

CHAPTER 3
Forgiving Others?

On a bright and sunny day, I had a call from Margarita. She wanted an appointment with me to share her situation with her husband. After hearing her story, I said:

Father: Margarita, I hear you feel very frustrated with your situation and that so far everything you have tried to do about it has not worked. You have gotten angry and even screamed at your husband, while at other times you have just tried to ignore his actions. You repented of your improper reactions. You have also tried the opposite, speaking kindly to him in hopes of developing a better relationship. But things have remained the same.

Margarita: Yes, Father, that's right. I don't know what else I can do. I don't want to be angry, but I can't control myself. I have tried to forgive him, but it has not worked. I don't feel the deep love towards him as I once had because he keeps doing the same things. I am depressed. I pray daily, for him and myself. I pray to have peace again, to forgive him and eventually to forget the hurt I feel. But I don't see any changes taking place in him or in me. What can I do? I am exhausted with this situation.

Father: Margarita, are you saying you want a solution and do not know what else you can do?

Margarita: Exactly. I don't know what to do.

Father: Margarita, it sounds like you want to do something that will produce better fruit in your life.

Margarita: That is right. Father, before we start, I want you to know I have invited Jesus Christ to be my Lord and Savior. I pray daily, especially for my husband and my children, but nothing seems to be changing; I don't see the results. Please help me. I want to have peace about this situation.

Father: Margarita, you said that you have accepted Jesus Christ into your life as your Lord and Savior. Let me ask you a question:

Why did Jesus die on the cross?

Margarita: To pay the price for our sins, to save us.

Father: Exactly, to remove our sins. But what are the sins He wants to destroy in us? There are two sins that deprive us of the freedom and the life He has for us. Do you know which ones they are?

Margarita: Mortal and venial sins.

Father: These are two degrees of sins, but what are the two sins that take away our peace, joy and the sense of an abundant life?

Margarita: I don't know, Father.

Father: Margarita, in the "Our Father," Jesus Christ taught us to pray His Kingdom come and His Will be done on earth as it is in heaven, saying: *"forgive us our trespasses as we forgive those who trespass against us."* These are the two sins for which Christ paid the price with His Blood, poured out on the cross to free us and give us new life: my sins and the sins of others; Jesus also paid for the consequences of sin. [cf. Rom. 5:9-10].

Jesus Christ wants us to receive His victory over these sins by the merits of His death and resurrection. When He died on the cross for these sins, Jesus gave us a victory that is free for the taking. What He wants from us is our acceptance of this victory through the repentance of our own sins, and the forgiveness of offenses and irritations of others. Our Father in Heaven loved the world so profoundly, Margarita, that He sent His only begotten Son to save us from all evil (John 3:16). Therefore, we are invited to accept this victory by receiving what He already won for us on the cross. We are invited to participate in His saving action by accepting what He has done so we may receive the victory which He won for us.

Some people think that because Christ won the victory for us, we don't have to do anything, except to believe. However if we truly believe that He won this victory, then we have to respond actively through repentance and forgiveness. Just as you did, we all must invite Jesus to be the Lord and Savior of our lives, which activates what we have already received through Baptism. Likewise, we must participate in this saving work by accepting and cooperating with our heavenly Father's grace, which He gives us by the merits of the death and resurrection of His Son, Jesus Christ, and by the presence and the power of the Holy Spirit.

So now, Margarita, what is the action we do when we forgive others? In other words, what does forgiveness mean to you? What do you do in order to forgive?

Margarita: I think forgiveness is that I forget the wrong the offender has done.

Father: By forgetting the offense, do you mean you will then act as if the other person did not do anything wrong?

Margarita: I suppose so, but I cannot do that. I have tried without success.

Father: I believe many people think like you, Margarita. I have also been told by others that for them to forgive is acting like the offense never took place or to find excuses for what the offender did. In either case, they are trying to invalidate their feelings of anger at being offended. Others have said to me that to forgive is a way of merely accepting the offense and saying: "what happened to me does not matter" or "the offense does not bother or irritate me anymore" and/or "I do not have any anger or resentment towards the offender."

There are people who believe forgiveness is a form of acceptance of the wrong others have done without expecting the offender to rectify his wrong or to change.

Still others say that to forgive is an act of love. Surely to forgive is an act of love, but what is the action I take when I forgive another?

All of these ways of looking at forgiveness, mentioned above, seem to imply that to forgive is an action of denying the hurt the offended person has experienced in order to be set truly free. Yet, this is not necessarily so. In my experience, these are not effective ways of looking at forgiveness. When we forgive we do not excuse or deny the offense, but acknowledge the wrong and surrender it to Jesus crucified. To forgive is an act of power in which we participate to bring Jesus' victory to myself and to this person through His death which conquered evil. I am participating in Jesus releasing the grace of healing to me and conversion to that person while awaiting the response of his free will.

In other words, to forgive others is not so much an action that I do. It is an action that Christ Jesus does and in which I cooperate with His grace. I cannot take away sin, neither mine nor theirs. When Christ died on the cross, He paid the price for sin. This price, which He paid through the shedding of His blood, was to rescue me from the kingdom of darkness and from my participation in that kingdom through my sins. This means that He wants actively to be our Savior, freeing us from sin and to be our Lord, leading and empowering us to follow Him on the path of life.

When I choose, as an act of the will and with His grace to forgive others in the name of Jesus, I am transferring the offenses or irritations to Jesus Christ on the cross.

The dictionary says, to forgive another means to let go of the bad experience or hold no resentment; it also means to cancel the debt someone has with you. So, now my question to you is, where does the offense or irritation go when we let it go? And how do we merely let it go? How do we do this?

What I am saying is that I proclaim to the person using my imagination: "I forgive you in the name of Jesus for…." This is how I let the offense go to Jesus on the cross where He has already paid the price. When I do this act consciously, in faith, I am believing that the evil is no longer in me. It is transferred to Jesus crucified, Who is destroying the damaging effect of this offense or irritation in me while healing me interiorly. At the same time, I am participating in the offender, through Jesus' mercy, being offered a special grace from the Lord to live a more virtuous life.

Many people forgive without knowing the action that has taken place. I think that even though they do not specifically know what forgiveness is, they might be transferring the evil to Jesus when they say they are forgiving. It seems obvious to them, it is like when I ask people, "What is walking?" and they say, "It's walking." They perceive it as something so obvious that they do not deem it necessary to explain it further. Others respond by saying that to walk is to move one's feet. Then, in attempt for them to go further in depth with the definition, I would be seated and move my feet as they had said. Then I would ask them, "Is this walking?" Rather frustrated they would tell me that one must be standing and moving his feet. So, I would stand up and begin to move my feet. Once more they would tell me that the action that I was doing, which was based on their description, was not walking. Later on, they gave me a fuller definition and said that walking is when one moves his body, putting one leg in front of the other, etc. Sometimes, therefore, it is difficult to precisely define what walking is because we naturally understand it without describing it. The same thing could happen with forgiveness.

Margarita, I will explain more about what forgiveness is in a few moments. My desire is that as I am explaining more about what it is, this will help you to forgive in such a way as to benefit you and give you more fully the peace that only Jesus can give. This action empowered by grace, allows Jesus to work more fully in you and through you for the well-being of others.

[As I was searching for some of my notes on my desk, Margarita was pondering on the words that I had just spoken to her, and then she said to me anxiously:]

Margarita: Father, please continue I am really interested in knowing more about forgiveness.

Father: It is important to know that we can forgive not only people, but also situations. These can also irritate or hurt us. Some examples of these are: "I can't find work; I have a flat tire; I am sick; a barking dog keeps me awake at night; etc."

Let me put this reality of forgiveness in another way: when we forgive in Jesus Christ's name, we are placing the irritation or offense upon Him, so He can defeat the wrong and its evil effect, namely to me and to the offender himself. Jesus Christ died on the cross to deliver us from all evil, but we have to choose consciously to transfer it into His hands and trust in His victory over evil. This action is freeing for myself, the one offended, while supporting the offender in God's work of transformation. This is Christian forgiveness.

Here is an image which might help you to better understand this action of forgiving. When I was a child, I played a game called "hot potato." When a group of people got in a circle and tossed a ball to one another they called out: "hot potato." The one who received this "hot potato" so as not to get burnt had to toss it to another person saying the same: "hot potato."

The Lord seemed to indicate to me how both repenting of my sins and forgiving those of another is like the game of "hot potato." I need to toss my sins or those of others to Jesus. It was like saying to each sin: "hot potato" or in other words: "this sin, mine or theirs, is too hot for me" so I toss the sin to Jesus. Essentially since these sins – mine or theirs – are too hot for me, I have to immediately toss them to Jesus trusting that my freedom lies in Him destroying the evil and empowering me to be more free. He does not want me to live under the burden of sin: neither mine nor theirs. Later we are going to see that the Sacrament of Reconciliation is Jesus' presence to help us to transfer these evils to Him for His victory.

Margarita: Father, now I see this differently. This is very helpful to understand better what true forgiveness is. Thank you. This will help me to actually forgive and experience greater freedom from the wrongs done to me. I especially liked the example of the "hot potato." This makes it more concrete for me.

My problem is that, at times, I don't want to forgive or I keep thinking that I can't forgive. If I do forgive, it doesn't seem to be authentic because I still feel the irritation towards the person or the situation. What can I do?

Father: Thank you, Margarita. I encourage you to forgive even when you do not want to do it or it seems inauthentic. To help you do that, I will explain the importance of forgiving others so that you would want to do it. After this, I will explain a method that will help you to forgive from the heart, which will help your forgiveness be more authentic.

Jesus Christ, in Matthew 6:12, teaches us how to pray to the Father with these words: *"And forgive us our debts, as we also have forgiven our debtors."*

Why is it so important to put these words into practice? Jesus tells us in Matthew 6:14-15: *"For if you forgive others their trespasses, your heavenly Father will also forgive you; but if you do not forgive others, neither will your Father forgive your trespasses."*

Jesus indicates that the forgiveness of others' offenses/irritations is necessary in order to obtain the remission of our sins because by not forgiving, we are actually sinning by judging and condemning them, holding on to their offenses. I believe He wants us to be aware of how, when we do not forgive others, we carry not only our sins, but also our sinful reactions or responses to the offenders' sins. Our reaction not to forgive is an added burden to our own sinful condition that existed beforehand. When we repent of our incorrect response and forgive the offender in the name of Jesus for what he has done wrong, Jesus is able to give us more life and the power to overcome our own sinful condition.

In the Gospel of Mark 11:24-25, Jesus indicates how in our prayers, forgiveness is connected to obtaining His favor in our other areas of necessity: *"So I tell you, whatever you ask for in prayer, believe that you have received it, and it will be yours. Whenever you stand praying, forgive, if you have anything against anyone; so that your Father in heaven may also forgive you your trespasses."*

In Luke 6:37, Jesus tells us we have to do something with the wrongdoings or the irritations that happen in our lives: *"Do not judge, and you will not be judged; do not condemn, and you will not be condemned. Forgive, and you will be forgiven."*

Our Lord Jesus Christ tells us neither to judge nor to condemn by thinking a person who has done us wrong cannot change and be redeemed. When we forgive, we participate in God's work, extending His grace to transform and heal the offended and participate in God's work in the offender's transformation. Therefore, God uses us in His work of healing ourselves, the offended, and transforming the offender. Thus, Jesus Himself, teaches us that to forgive others is essential and beneficial for both.

In the above passage Jesus tells us that there are three types of reactions that we could have toward a person who offends or irritates us: to judge, to condemn or to forgive. What Jesus wants of us, for our own good and that of the world, is for us to choose to forgive and when we do, to forgive from the heart. In Matthew 18:32-35, Jesus teaches us about this with the parable of the unforgiving debtor. *"Then his Lord summoned him and said to him; 'You wicked slave! I forgave you all that debt because you pleaded with me. Should you not have had mercy on your fellow-slave, as I had mercy on you?' And in anger his lord handed him over to be tortured until he should pay his entire debt. So my heavenly Father will also do to every one of you, if you do not forgive your brother or sister from your heart."*

Now you are ready to learn the process of how to achieve forgiveness from the heart which only happens with the help of God's grace, the fruit of His living presence within us.

Margarita: I am ready to learn how to apply forgiveness to my situation, so I can be free from the burden of these offenses and irritations. I also want to participate in helping my husband with his condition, which seems impossible for me to endure any longer.

Father: Before I explain more it is good to note, if you want the act of forgiving continually to benefit you, that it is important daily for several weeks or longer to seek God's grace to practice a method of forgiveness like this one. Then it can become a habit, a new way of responding as a more natural and instinctive reaction to every person and situation, thus becoming a part of your way of living. It is also best, if possible, to practice this approach in a place where there is the least amount of external distractions.

The Lord Jesus Christ has taught us in Mathew 6 how there are times we must go to a private place so we can communicate in a profound way with our heavenly Father. This can be applied to forgiveness, by closing the door to as many outside distractions as possible. I say this because when we start a prayer program, the adversary tries to cause all kinds of interruptions, for example someone coming at the door or the phone ringing during your prayer time. Also, for certain situations and people, such as family members, it is necessary to take time alone with the Lord so that the act of forgiveness may produce a more profound result. Forgiveness from the heart, being a serious activity, also necessitates a special preparation and proper environment, so it can produce its deep effect in us. Also, when we want to do something from the heart, deep within ourselves, it usually takes time.

Another important element necessary to forgive from the heart is to forgive in the name of Jesus Christ, Who has died and is risen. Jesus Christ, when He healed the paralytic, told him his sins were forgiven, but the Pharisees said that only God can forgive sins. Jesus Christ did not deny this, but by healing the man, He showed that, as the Son of Man, He had the power to forgive sin. In this, Jesus manifested He was God. Jesus taught us in the "Our Father" that we are to forgive those who offend us. To achieve this, we must forgive in His name. And through this we are transferring it [like a "hot potato"] to Him because only Jesus can truly forgive or take away sin. He will then work through us to transform us [the offended], and the offender.

It is also important to remember the following:

THE ACT OF FORGIVENESS FROM THE HEART HAS THREE BASIC ASPECTS WHICH ARE INCLUDED IN THE SEVEN STEPS OF FORGIVING FROM THE HEART

1. RECOGNIZE the offense or irritation and all the emotions that it produced when it occurred;

2. PROCLAIM in the name of Jesus, in your mind, the words of forgiveness and blessing over the offender. In this way you TRANSFER the offense or irritation TO JESUS, on His cross where He won the victory.

3. TRUST FIRMLY WITH UNWAVERING FAITH that the Lord through His Holy Spirit is transforming the offense or irritation into an action of freeing you from this evil and helping the offender in his process of conversion so as freely to choose the Lord's ways.

After these three aspects, you need to show love to the person, the offender, in the way the Lord indicates so as to further participate in the Lord's transforming work in that person.

In the following pages I will further explain the seven steps that will help you forgive from the heart in the name of Jesus. Each step will have a prayer relating to forgiveness and then there will be an explanation regarding each of the seven steps. If you have a question over what I just explained, let me know, because I want you to understand everything as fully as possible.

Margarita: It is becoming clearer to me. Thank you. I can't wait to learn more.

CHAPTER 4

Preparation Steps for Forgiving Others

Father: Let us now talk about the first three steps that will prepare you to forgive from the heart. The preparation steps can be done as you begin your day or just before proclaiming forgiveness toward the person or situation. Practicing these preparation steps first thing in the morning will help you to forgive with greater ease at the time of the offense. Just like taking a vitamin pill in the morning, it will protect and keep your defenses strong throughout the day.

Nevertheless, when a strong infection occurs, we need to take further action. When the offense or irritation is more intense, one would benefit from repeating the three preparation steps followed by the other four steps in the forgiveness process.

1. ASK FOR THE PRESENCE OF THE HOLY SPIRIT:

A recommended prayer:

God, our Father, fill me with Your Holy Spirit and give me the grace that empowers me to forgive from the heart. Do this by means of the merits of the death and resurrection of Your Son, Jesus. I want You, Father, to be glorified through this forgiveness.

Come Holy Spirit, come, through the powerful intercession of Mary, Your beloved Spouse. I receive You into my life at this moment. I imagine Your coming as a light that is filling a dark room. I thank You, Holy Spirit, for coming to me with such strength. [Pause to be conscious of this presence.]

This prayer imploring the presence of the Holy Spirit can be shorter; for example, you can simply say: **Come Holy Spirit, and help me to forgive from my heart. Thank You for Your presence.** [Pause to be conscious of this presence.]

I like to implore the Father for His gift of the Holy Spirit as Jesus tells us in Luke 11: 11-13: "*Is there anyone among you who, if your child asks for a fish, will give a snake instead of a fish? Or if the child asks for an egg, will give a scorpion? If you then, who are evil, know how to give good gifts to your children; how much more will the heavenly Father give the Holy Spirit to those who ask him!*"

The passage states we should ask for the Holy Spirit from the heavenly Father. Thus, in this prayer I ask the Father for the Holy Spirit. I add through the merits of Jesus' death and resurrection because of what John the Baptist said in Luke 3:16, as he proclaimed how Jesus would baptize us with the Holy Spirit: "*John answered all of them by saying, 'I baptize you with water; but one who is more powerful than I is coming; I am not worthy to untie the thong of his sandals. He will baptize you with the Holy Spirit and fire.*"

There are many prayers and songs directly addressed to the Holy Spirit. In Latin there is one famous prayer that is called 'Veni Creator Spiritus' - Come, Creator Spirit. The crucial element is for us to have a sense of the Holy Spirit giving us the power to forgive from the heart and to be aware that He comes from the Father through His Son, Jesus Christ.

The Holy Spirit formed Jesus in His humanity within the womb of the Blessed Virgin Mary. It was through her "yes" that the Holy Spirit did this marvelous work of giving us our Savior, Jesus Christ. His main work, in the descriptions given to us through Scriptures and the Church, is the continuous forming of Jesus within each of us. He does this by helping us to know the Father, to pray and to be true witnesses of Jesus. The Father began this transferring action of sending His Son through the Holy Spirit in Mary, who had given her consent for this work. Mary is, therefore, the spouse of the Holy Spirit. She is still the spouse of the Holy Spirit who formed Jesus in His humanity. Jesus, through this human body, is forming a new body, a mystical body, of which we are members. Mary is still His mother even in this new mystical body, which He is forming. For these reasons, it is good to include this great mystery of Mary, as spouse of the Holy Spirit. They have not divorced. We ask her to be present to help us receive the Holy Spirit forming Jesus as our Savior and Lord within us. So in my prayer, I like to say: **Come Holy Spirit by means of the powerful intercession of Mary, Your well-beloved spouse.**

In another passage, Matthew 7:7, Jesus tells us that when we ask, we receive. It is valuable not only to ask that He come, but also to receive in faith what He has specifically promised, His Holy Spirit. The two ways I use to receive the Holy Spirit in faith are: 1) thanking Him for being present because of my invitation according to His word and 2) using my imagination to picture what I am requesting as occurring. In both ways, I proclaim that because of my faith in His word, I receive the Holy Spirit and I do so visualizing it, for example, as a light filling a dark room, and by thanking Him for His presence for which I have been petitioning.

Margarita: Father, if we already received the Holy Spirit when we were baptized, why do we have to ask for the Holy Spirit again? Is this not doubting that we already have Him?

Father: Margarita, thank you for your question. We have the Holy Spirit from our Baptism, but when we ask again, we are acknowledging we still are in need of His active presence in every activity of our lives. It is also a way, in this concrete situation of forgiveness, to reaffirm and be conscious that we are in need of Him in a very special way in order to forgive from the heart and not merely with words. I never tire of asking for the Holy Spirit's presence in everything that happens in my life. I recognize I am nothing without God and I need His help always. My experience has been that the Holy Spirit helps me more when I do this than when I don't. It is an act of humility in which I recognize how, without Him, I am nothing and can do nothing.

Besides, forgiving originates from a divine action [only God can forgive sin] and a command to us from the Lord *["Forgive, and you will be forgiven."* Luke 6:37]. Thus in order for me to participate in the action of forgiving, as He requests, I need the grace of God through the Holy Spirit.

Margarita: Thank you, Father. This explanation helps me a lot. Now I understand.

Father: Conscious of the Holy Spirit's presence, the second and third preparation steps help us be more aware of two realties of God which are very helpful in the process of forgiving from the heart.

2. BE CONSCIOUS THAT GOD LOVES BOTH YOU AND THE OTHER PERSON(S) WHO NEEDS TO BE FORGIVEN

After seeking the Holy Spirit's presence, I suggest you pray something like the following prayer:

Father, You are marvelous. You sent Your Son, Jesus Christ, to show us Your mercy. I praise You for this love, manifested in His coming as one of us: to live with us, to teach us, to die to pay the price for our sins, to rise to a new life for us, and to send the Holy Spirit to us. I thank You for Your presence here with me to help me to forgive the offenses or irritations of... [Mention here the name(s) of the person(s) or the situation(s)]. **Thank You because You want to save them and me from all sin and all evil.**

In Matthew 5:42-48, Jesus Christ taught us that we are to love our enemies: *"Give to everyone who begs from you, and do not refuse anyone who wants to borrow from you. You have heard that it was said, 'You shall love your neighbor and hate your enemy.' But I say to you, 'Love your enemies and pray for those who persecute you, so that you may be children of your Father in heaven; for he makes his sun rise on the evil and on the good, and sends rain on the righteous and on the unrighteous. For if you love those who love you, what reward do you have? Do not even the tax-collectors do the same? And if you greet only your brothers and sisters, what more are you doing than others? Do not even the Gentiles do the same? Be perfect, therefore, as your heavenly Father is perfect.'"*

And in Luke 6: 37 He says: *"Do not judge, and you will not be judged; do not condemn, and you will not be condemned. Forgive, and you will be forgiven."*

To love those who have offended you, it is essential first to receive consciously and deeply the love of God so as to be able to forgive from the heart. It is immensely powerful to understand and accept that God loves us both: the offended and the offender, with an infinite and eternal love, as Jeremiah 31:3 says: *"I have loved you with an everlasting love; therefore I have continued my faithfulness to you."* Also, 1John 4:8 reminds us that *"God is love."* To forgive others is a way to love the way He loved us, just as Jesus prayed for his persecutors on the cross: *"Father, forgive them; for they do not know what they are doing."* Therefore, to forgive others, it is most helpful to receive consciously the depths of His love.

Margarita: Father, I know He loves me, but how do I receive His love more deeply?

Father: Margarita, to receive His love more deeply first you need to be convinced of the truth of His word whether circumstances are in your favor or not. Take for example the truth of His word as in Isaiah 43:1-4a, *"But now thus says the LORD, he who created you, O Jacob, he who formed you, O Israel: Do not fear, for I have redeemed you; I have called you by name, you are mine. When you pass through the waters, I will be with you; and through the rivers, they shall not overwhelm you; when you walk through fire you shall not be burned, and the flame shall not consume you. For I am the LORD your God, the Holy One of Israel, your Saviour. I give Egypt as your ransom, Ethiopia and Seba in exchange for you. Because you are precious in my sight, and honored, and I love you, I give people in return for you, nations in exchange for your life."* And in John 15:13 Jesus reminds us of His love when He says: *"No one has greater love than this, to lay down one's life for one's friends."*

Next, to receive His love more profoundly, it would help you to take into your hands a crucifix, or any other image of Jesus Christ or Mary that expresses His love for you, and gaze upon it while repeating a passage from Scriptures of His love, such as Jeremiah 31:3 *"I have loved you with an everlasting love; therefore I have continued my faithfulness to you."* You could also use another passage speaking of God's love such as quoted in the above paragraph. With these passages of the Lord expressing His love for me, I put on His lips my name (e.g. Francis), because as in Isaiah 43:1 He says *"I call you by name."* For a few minutes pause while continuing to gaze upon the image and repeat these words, while thanking Him until they start to resound deeply within you.

Remember you are not alone in this. The Holy Spirit is present to move you more towards this reality of God's love, which goes beyond what the mind can capture as we read in Ephesians 3:19: *"...and to know the love of Christ that surpasses knowledge, so that you may be filled with all the fullness of God."*

God's love is unconditional. When you receive His love more deeply, you can more easily forgive from the heart in the name of Jesus.

Receiving His love when you are offended or irritated will also help you know that God is with you in your pain. Every suffering you have, Jesus Himself has also suffered and is now suffering with you. He wants you to come with your suffering united to His so that He can give you His victory. It will help you to express to the Father how much the offense(s) and/or irritation(s) affects you. You don't want to deny the pain you feel as you offer it to Him and receive His love.

Margarita: Thank you, Father; I am going to add this practice to my daily personal prayer time. I think often I am unable to forgive, because I am not sufficiently aware of the depth of His love for me. I need the power of the Holy Spirit to help me receive His love deeply and to know He loves the other person also. When my feelings of hatred, resentment, anger or frustration against someone are deep, it is hard to accept God's grace to love and forgive the offender.

Father: This is a very good point Margarita. First receive His love for you, and then accept intellectually that the Lord also loves the other person(s), because He created them. Don't force it beyond that. This will get you started to love with God's love. The next preparation step will also continue to help you.

3. RECEIVE GOD'S MERCY

Prayer: **God our Father, help me to see my sins and to remember the mercy You have shown me.**

[Take a moment Margarita to remember your past sins and the many times He has forgiven you. Seek the forgiveness of God if you remember sins for which you have not yet asked and received His forgiveness. Also, this is the time to ask for forgiveness for your own sinful ways either in your mind or externally in words or action of responding to one who wronged or irritated you. We need to be honest before the Lord with sins we have committed and take advantage of this moment to pray and receive His forgiveness, His mercy.]

Jesus, please forgive me and wash me with Your precious Blood that You shed to save me from all my sins and from the tendency to repeat these evils.

Take enough time, Margarita, so as to have an interior conviction of this grace of His forgiveness towards you. One way to do this is to imagine yourself inside a circle of light. In this Divine presence, allow the Lord to touch your heart with His forgiving, merciful love.

We have a God of mercy. He knows we are imperfect and weak. He does not condemn us but wants to rescue us from our faults, weaknesses, and our tendencies towards sin. John 3:17 says: *"Indeed, God did not send the Son into the world to condemn the world, but in order that the world might be saved through him."*

Margarita: Father, I may be taking you away from your explanation of the steps of forgiveness, but it is important for me to ask: how does one know what is sinful? Can you clarify how I can know what is right and what is wrong (evil)? The reason I am asking you is because some people say that what is "good" is what one feels is "good" or what the majority of people say, or what my family, society and/or school have taught us is "good." If I were to do the opposite of these, they would say I would be doing evil. Therefore, your explanation will help me to know what to forgive if I do not feel an irritation but that person has sinned or done what is wrong before God. It will also help me to know if I need to repent of something that I was not aware of as sinful.

Father: Let me try to clarify some things briefly, regarding this. As Christians, we believe God is the Creator of the world. He established an order for the entire universe, including us as human beings. We have special gifts, namely, a mind and a free will which enable us to understand and make choices. As human beings, we can choose to obey God's plan or not. God is our Creator, and as such He has given us His plan through His commandments. By obeying them, we can be what He made us to be, namely, a fully alive human being. He gives us the freedom to choose good or evil, but He wants us to choose His ways because He wants us to have life. This is explained in Deuteronomy 30:15-20: *"See, I have set before you today life and prosperity, death and adversity. If you obey the commandments of the LORD your God that I am commanding you today, by loving the LORD your God, walking in his ways, and observing his commandments, decrees, and ordinances, then you shall live and become numerous, and the LORD your God will bless you in the land that you are entering to possess. But if your heart turns away and you do not hear, but are led astray to bow down to other gods and serve them, I declare to you today that you shall perish; you shall not live long in the land that you are crossing the Jordan to enter and possess. I call heaven and earth to witness against you today that I have set before you life and death, blessings and curses. Choose life so that you and your descendants may live, loving the LORD your God, obeying him, and holding fast to him; for that means life to you and length of days, so that you may live in the land that the LORD swore to give to your ancestors, to Abraham, to Isaac, and to Jacob."*

In Isaiah 55:8-9 the Lord reminds us: *"For my thoughts are not your thoughts, nor are your ways my ways, says the LORD. For as the heavens are higher than the earth, so are my ways higher than your ways and my thoughts than your thoughts."*

Thus God reveals to us what is right, proper and life-giving. If we do not do this, it creates disorder and disharmony in us and in our environment. This can be found in a powerful way in Sacred Scriptures, both in the Old and New Testaments, where we have the Commandments, established by God, which give us life. He gives us these so that we can be fully alive human beings, as Irenaeus, one of the Church Fathers declares.

If one has any confusion as to what is right and wrong, Jesus Christ also left us His authority in the Church to teach with clarity what is right and what is wrong for us. He did this when He said that listening to the Church is listening to Him.

This is found in Luke 10:16: *"Whoever listens to you listens to me, and whoever rejects you rejects me, and whoever rejects me rejects the one who sent me."*

To make this even clearer, Jesus promised to be with His Church under the direction of His apostles with Peter as their leader, and their successors until the end of time. Matthew 28:19-20: *"Go therefore and make disciples of all nations, baptizing them in the name of the Father and of the Son and of the Holy Spirit, and teaching them to obey everything that I have commanded you. And remember, I am with you always, to the end of the age."*

Through the Bible and His Church Jesus wants His will, what is right and what is wrong, to be clear. There are different situations that arise today which need to be clarified by the Church because the Bible does not directly address them. This is the case, for example, with contraceptives. The Church has needed to state clearly that contraceptives are not God's plan for man and woman. The idea of this namely, not being of God, is implied in the Bible in such passages as Genesis 1:28, *"be fruitful and multiply..."*

Jesus' will is made very clear by the teachings of the Pope, the successor to Peter and appointed head of His Church, with specific authority to act in His name. We read in Matthew 16:17-19, where Christ promised to guide the Church through the leadership of Peter and his successors, the Popes of the Church: *"And Jesus answered him, 'Blessed are you, Simon son of Jonah! For flesh and blood has not revealed this to you, but my Father in heaven. And I tell you, you are Peter, and on this rock I will build my church, and the gates of Hades will not prevail against it. I will give you the keys of the kingdom of heaven, and whatever you bind on earth will be bound in heaven, and whatever you loose on earth will be loosed in heaven."*

The Catechism of the Catholic Church [in Part Three: Life in Christ, Section 2, Chapter 1] tells us that since the time of the apostles, the Church's function, under the promises of Jesus, has been to guide and direct His Church as to what we are to believe or what we are to do or not to do so as to be faithful to Jesus and His will for us. We read in 1 Timothy 3:14-15, *"I hope to come to you soon, but I am writing these instructions to you so that, if I am delayed, you may know how one ought to behave in the household of God, which is the church of the living God, the pillar and bulwark of the truth."*

Margarita, it is necessary for you to compare your life with what He has revealed to us in order to see if you are choosing what is God's will. The Lord, Creator of the universe, is our only Guide to show us and to keep us on the path of what is right and what is wrong as manifested through His Church and the Bible. We are blessed to have the Catechism of the Catholic Church. This helps us hear Jesus through His Church to know what to believe, and to know what is right and wrong as revealed through the Sacred Scriptures and confirmed and clarified through the Church which Jesus established.

When we sin, choosing a path different from the one He has revealed, Jesus invites us to repent. When another person chooses a path different from the one He has revealed, Jesus wants us to forgive him/her. He came to rescue us from all evil and its manifestations and to guide us in the path of true life and freedom.

Through His Holy Spirit Jesus calls us to repent and walk in His ways by placing our sins on His cross where He forgives us and transforms us. However, we need to accept this victory of Jesus Christ in faith, faith in His word. Let us remember what 1 John 1:9 says: *"If we confess our sins, he who is faithful and just will forgive us our sins and cleanse us from all unrighteousness."* Through the action of His Holy Spirit, He empowers us to live in conformity with Him and His will for us.

54

Margarita: Thank you, Father. I think I understand better what is right and what is wrong and where I can find out more about this. This will help me to know when something is wrong, so I can forgive others their offenses. I also see how knowing what is right and wrong helps me to be aware of my own sins and, repenting of these, allows me to be more merciful to others.

Father: Exactly! Margarita, it is also good to remember that, as human beings, we have the tendency to see evil in others more than in ourselves.

Here are a couple examples of the importance of repenting of my sins when someone has done something wrong or I perceive it as wrong:

One is when we are angry, disgusted or frustrated with someone else, we often do not notice our own reactions toward the offender. When the Holy Spirit reveals our need to repent of our incorrect reaction, whether expressed interiorly or exteriorly, it is then easier to forgive the offender. An example of this would be when we react by ignoring, by accusing, or by belittling the person who offends us. These types of reactions need our repentance and receiving Christ's mercy toward us before we forgive what was offensive or irritating in that person.

Another example is when we are doing almost the same thing as the one who is offending us but in a little different way and we do not want to recognize this. We need enough humility to ask the Holy Spirit to help us to see if this is so, in order that we can repent and change our own defects. Then we are ready to forgive what we perceive as wrong in that person. An example of this latter might be when we live with an alcoholic and yet we act similarly in our response to the alcoholic person and to others but we do not want to recognize this.

Note: it is also important to take care not to think when someone has done something wrong that it does not irritate or bother me so I do not need to forgive that person. When someone does something offensive I need to forgive them for my own benefit and the good of the one(s) who was offensive.

Margarita, as we know, part of the process of forgiving another is to repent. To understand better the impact our repentance has on the transformation of others, let me share a testimony with you. There were some religious sisters who had two lots of land on which they were planning to build an orphanage. However, their properties were separated by a lot where an elderly woman lived.

It was necessary to have this land to join their two lots in order to build an orphanage. So they went to visit the lady, but she would neither sell nor give it to them. They prayed for her. They also visited her frequently so as to continue their friendship. Though she did not have heirs to which she could leave her property, she would not consider selling the lot to them. One day, a newly appointed religious sister came to reside with them. She decided to visit the elderly lady since she was a new arrival. When she rang the doorbell, a little girl greeted her at the door and invited her to come in. The girl explained that the lady went shopping. The girl invited her to come into her home. None of the other sisters had ever gone inside. This religious sister noticed the lady had accumulated many mattresses; there were about ten in two of the bedrooms. When she returned to the convent, she shared with her sisters, who concluded, the lady had a problem with greed.

In the following weeks, the sisters asked the Lord to help them become conscious of the ways they too were greedy. They began to see greed in their own lives even though it was in minute ways. They repented and made changes in their lives. After a while, they visited the lady again, and they noticed that the lady responded to them with more joy. And to their surprise, the lady asked them if they still wanted her lot. She then proceeded to ask them if she gave it to them, could she continue to live in the house until she died and have the plums from her trees. The sisters, of course, said yes, and the woman agreed to give them the lot so that they could start preparing the construction plans for the orphanage.

You see, sometimes, it is necessary to repent of vices similar to the ones of the person offending or irritating us, even though they may not be as grave, for the offender's greater transformation. This could also give us a deeper freedom from the irritation he/she has caused.

CHAPTER 5

The Final Steps in Forgiving Others

Father: Margarita, now let's examine the next steps in the process of forgiving from the heart. These steps involve both forgiving and receiving the fruit of forgiveness.

4. FORGIVE AND BLESS IN THE NAME OF JESUS

Take one person or situation at a time unless several people with the same offense are involved. An example of several people involved in the same offense might be when one has had an abortion. Here were several people who participated in this evil: the father, the mother of the child, those who encouraged them to have the abortion, the receptionist, the nurses and doctors, etc. In this case, you could forgive them as a group rather than individually in regards to the same offense.

The value of forgiving one at a time, unless several were involved in the same offense, is that each person and situation is given the time they need in order for the healing power of forgiveness to take effect within you and within that person or situation who caused the offense and/or irritation.

Then with each individual [or, as in the above cases, each group] pray while imagining you both of you at the foot of the cross where evil was conquered:

Father, surround this person(s) (or situation) with the light of Your presence and love. And Father, I thank You for Your infinite mercy for him/her/them.

[Then, take a moment to visualize the person(s) surrounded with the light of Christ and then, out loud or in your mind, but preferably not face to face, continue with:] **And in the name of our Lord Jesus Christ I forgive**

you for... [Take time to mention the offense or fault while being conscious of any feelings that may have been present at the time of the offense or irritation]. **And I give thanks that I have now forgiven you in the name of Jesus. This offense is now on His cross where it is being conquered. Amen.**

And in the name of our Lord Jesus Christ, I bless you with... [Mention the particular blessing you think this person or situation needs to be more like what Jesus wants the person to be]. **And I give thanks because you are now being blessed by Jesus. Amen.** [As I proclaim that it is done and say "Amen," I acknowledge that I have done my part to transfer this offense to Jesus, as best I could under the power and presence of the Holy Spirit, His grace. I have fulfilled what Jesus asked, namely, to forgive so I can be forgiven. As a I say Amen, I am confident that Jesus is now working what He was doing before I forgave to deepen the transformation of that person while honoring his free will.]

Margarita, Jesus Christ taught us to be merciful as He is merciful to those who sin (Luke 6:36). He cancels our debt when He forgives our sins. We deserve death, but Jesus paid the price to set us free from sin and death. His forgiveness is available for us whenever with sorrow we repent of our sins and allow Him to lead us in new ways. Jesus wants us, through His forgiveness to us, to do the same to others who have offended or irritated us.

Here is an example of what I am trying to say regarding showing mercy because we have received so much mercy from the Lord. In the Old Testament, the just man sins seven* times a day (Proverbs 24:16). Imagine a highly just person sinning three times a day. In one year (365 days), he sinned more than 1,000 times. If he is 27 years old and we don't count the first seven years, he sinned at least 20,000 times. The Lord forgave his 20,000 sins when he repented. How much more should we forgive one, two or several offenses from the one who offends us? We have received so much mercy so as to give mercy.

*[Note: the number seven in the Bible, as other numbers, is rich with symbolism. It means perfection or fullness. So when it is said of the 'Just',

(in other words, the one who follows God's commandments), that he sins seven times' this means that sin is still a part of his life, that he falls often. But I am using seven in this example as if it were meant in a literal sense so as to show how merciful the Lord is with us.]

St. Faustina in her diary described three things the Lord wants us to do in order to receive His mercy continually:

- To ask for God's mercy regularly for our offenses against the Lord;

- To trust in His mercy [which means when we sin and repent of our sins He pays the price and sets us free to walk in a new way with Him];

- To be merciful to others as He is merciful to us.

In Latin, the word for mercy is miseri-cor-dia, "cor =heart". Thus, mercy has the implication that the action involves one's heart; it is a heart filled action toward a person in the misery of his/her sinfulness. It is what God gives us, in His infinite love for us, when He pays for our sins even before we repent, even though we do not deserve it (cf. Rom. 5:8). This mercy gives us the opportunity to repent so as to experience His newness of life within ourselves. This same mercy is what He wants us to have for others, so we can receive His continuous and abundant mercy. This also enables the Lord more easily to bring the other to repentance.

As I said earlier it is best to forgive one person at a time, to make this action more personal, except when several persons committed the same offense. Another example of this would be a case when someone has had sexual relations with various people. It is important for the person first to repent of his/her own sins and to forgive each one individually. However, they could all be forgiven as a group especially if there is no particular remembrance of each individual. Sometimes we think it is enough to repent of our sins only. However, we also need to forgive all who participated in our sin in that we not only sinned, but, by participating with us in this sin, they also sinned against us. The act of repenting and forgiving will free us from our sins, also the impact of the sins of others who sinned with us, giving us a total freedom from our sins. It is also good, as Neal Lozano says in his book, *Unbound*, interiorly to take back in the name of Jesus the authority we gave the person in this act. [Cf. pp. 252-254.]

Margarita, another benefit in forgiving the other person who shared in your sin is to break the chains you have with that person and reestablish your dignity as a son/daughter of God. I do not refer exclusively to sexual offenses, but also to any other sin, such as getting drunk with someone else, stealing, abortion [for example, as I mentioned earlier, the father, anyone who encouraged the abortion, the receptionist, the doctor, the nurses, etc.], in other words, with others who participated with you in the evil. When you forgive the other person, you receive more victory because not only through repentance is your sin removed, but through this forgiveness the wrong of the other person will not remain in you but it will be on the cross where Jesus destroys within you the power of both your sin and theirs.

Margarita: Wow, I never thought of this. Now I am aware of additional people I need to forgive.

And so what should I do if I am not sure I have forgiven someone?

Father: Sometimes when you are not certain you have forgiven or not forgiven from the heart, it would be helpful to forgive again so as to be more certain. Forgiveness never hurts anyone but benefits both you and the other(s).

There are many people we have not forgiven. These irritations or offenses remain within us. I remember a woman who shared with me what she did when she discovered the power of forgiveness. She wanted to return to her past to be sure she had forgiven past offenses. She divided her life into four sections: the first one, from conception to five years old; the second one, from six to twelve years old; the third section from thirteen to nineteen years old; and the last one from twenty to fifty or more years old.

The worst evils, the ones that affect us most deeply, happen when we were younger and more vulnerable.

After dividing her life into these sections, she took a week for each section and asked the Holy Spirit to reveal what had happened during these times. She made a list of people, and situations, which she wanted consciously to forgive from the heart. She obtained extraordinary results as she took time to forgive each person and situation.

I, imitating her, have practiced this exercise with forgiveness, and it helped me tremendously. Through the inspiration of the Holy Spirit, I came up with a list of people and situations I was not sure I had forgiven from the heart. I forgave and blessed them in the name of Jesus using the seven steps of forgiving from the heart. I found it was worth the time it took. What freedom this gave me!

Margarita: I cannot wait to try to do this myself. I know I still have a number of people to forgive as well as many situations. I often wondered why I had so much trouble with my quick temper. I can now see how carrying a lack of forgivness for so many past hurts could be the root of my angry reactions. I am not free of their offenses.

Father: This is something I also discovered.

When a volcano has too much activity inside, it is at the point of erupting. This is what was happening in me when I had accumulated anger. Then one more irritation or offense caused me quickly to get angry.

For example, when I was a child, I was not aware of the importance of forgiving those who hurt me. I did not forgive them from the heart because I did not understand what it meant to do this. No one had taught me how to forgive in a way I could understand. It was merely a word that I used at times rather than a process occurring deep within me.

What I found interesting is that in this whole process of forgiveness, the Lord is showing me still more people and situations that need my forgiveness. He wants me to be free of all the past evils and the disorders they produced in my life.

So when I have an angry reaction, stronger than the situation would normally deserve, it is probably due to past hurts that still need to be forgiven.

The Holy Spirit is always available to help us through this, so remember to implore His help, his grace. He wants us to be recipients of the victory which Christ, through His blood, won for us so as to rescue us from all evil.

Again, to forgive involves these three basic elements after preparing to forgive from the heart:

1. RECOGNIZE the offense or irritation with all the emotions that it produced when it happened.

2. PROCLAIM, in the name of Jesus Christ, the words of forgiveness and blessings over the offender in your mind, and thus TRANSFER the offense and/or irritation TO JESUS on His cross where He won the victory.

3. TRUST FIRMLY WITH UNWAVERING FAITH that the Lord who rose from the dead [victorious over sins and sickness] is through His Holy Spirit transforming the offense or irritation, freeing you of this evil and helping the offender in his process of conversion.

After these three steps, you need to make the decision to love the person in the way the Lord indicates so as to further participate in the Lord's transforming work in that person. This needs to flow from the forgiveness process and could even be considered a fourth element in this process.

When you say: In the name of our Lord Jesus Christ I forgive you for [name the offense], it is vital to proclaim in faith with words of gratitude that it is done, concluding with "Amen," which means it is so. Again this merely means that I have done what He asks of me by transferring consciously these offenses to Jesus Christ who is freeing me of their evil effect. He is also continuing His work of mercy towards the offender.

To forgive requires the mind to recognize the evil or the offense at the time it actually happened with whatever emotion was connected to it. Then our will must choose to transfer the evil to Jesus Christ, on the cross, where He poured out His Blood to free us.

When we think of a past evil done against us, the emotion can be unpleasant. Yet on occasion with some offenses, there can be little to no emotional reaction connected to it. If this happens, thank God because it is a special grace.

However, I know people who even feel positive emotions/reactions towards the offender, but have not consciously forgiven him/her. Forgiveness is a conscious act of transferring an evil to the Lord with the conviction that the Lord is liberating you from all damaging effects of the evil or irritation. It is not good to keep the evil within, saying we do not need to forgive the person. It is healthy to go through this process of forgiving from the heart consciously even when, with the passage of time, we do not have any feelings against the person.

Margarita: I did not realize that I must forgive even if I don't have anger or resentment towards the offender, especially when it does not seem that grave.

Father: Margarita, remember: to forgive never hurts us or anyone else. It is a blessing for the offender as well as the offended. Many people try to convince themselves and me that it is not necessary to forgive in some circumstances. I prefer to forgive rather than not to forgive. I do this even for the most insignificant things, in those that might be mere irritations. I want Jesus to free me from all that could rob me of His peace and victory.

When we forgive, we are not judging or condemning the offender, rather, both of us are being liberated from the evil effects produced by the offense even when it might have been something seemingly insignificant. The advantage of doing this regularly, for all forms of irritations or offenses, is that it forms a healthy and life-giving habit which can become a natural and spontaneous reaction to evils or perceived evils. Remember what Jesus Christ said, in Luke 6:37-38: *"Do not judge, and you will not be judged; do not condemn, and you will not be condemned. Forgive, and you will be forgiven; give, and it will be given to you. A good measure, pressed down, shaken together, running over, will be put into your lap; for the measure you give will be the measure you get back."*

When we judge or condemn, we have evaluated the person's motive and we are saying indirectly that they cannot change. Instead, when we forgive we are not evaluating the gravity of the offense nor how culpable the person is nor the grace that the person might have received to resist the temptation. We are transferring to Jesus the offense so as to bring His transformation to both the offended and the offender. People often say that they do not want to judge another, and so they do nothing with the evil. In this way they are actually approving the evil. Jesus wants us, however, always to forgive.

Also, it is worth remembering again that we often perceive something to be an offense, when in reality it may not be so, but because we think it is so, it would be best to forgive. An example would be: if you think someone in your family does not love you, it may not be a reality but only your perception. Another situation to forgive might be when someone thinks that someone has cursed them. In these cases, it is best to forgive in the name of Jesus Christ what you perceive as a wrong, so as to free yourself from the possible evil and offer a blessing in the name of Jesus Christ for that person. Sending a concrete blessing is always beneficial.

Margarita: Thank you, Father, for your explanation. I now see more clearly the necessity of forgiving because I did not forgive in this way. You mentioned we are to bless the person who has done some wrong or irritated us as part of the process of forgiveness. How can I do this?

Father: Thank you, Margarita, for using the term 'process' to describe the act of forgiveness since it is not a word or a moment, but a process that normally requires time and several important steps. Though with less serious offenses, the process could be shorter. An example of a less serious offense might be when someone drives irresponsibly. You could merely proclaim in the presence of the Holy Spirit step 4, which is to proclaim in the name of Jesus forgiveness and blessing to the offender. This may not be sufficient if the offense or irritation is deeper.

To answer your question, the blessing after forgiving is like having taken away something, namely, the offense or irritation, but it needs to be replaced with what the offender lacks to be a better person. Suppose someone offends me by being arrogant. I can bless the person saying: "In the name of Jesus Christ I bless you with the power to be more humble."

I remember a case where a child was angry with his mother because she was impatient and corrected him unjustly. She had not investigated what happened and presuming the worst, she began screaming at her son. In this case, after forgiving his mother, the child could say: "I bless you in the name of Jesus with the power to be more patient and to take time to find out what actually happens in each particular situation." In 1Peter 3:9 we hear the importance of a blessing at the time of an offense: *"Do not repay evil for evil or abuse for abuse* [even internally, in your mind]; *but on the contrary, repay with a blessing. It is for this that you were called--that you might inherit a blessing."*

In Luke 6:27-28 Christ also says: *"But I say to you that listen, Love your enemies, do good to those who hate you, bless those who curse you, pray for those who abuse you."*

To bless a person is to send, from your mind, something good that the offending person needs according to your point of view. Do it in the name of Jesus Christ. How often do we want to see another change! Many times we desire this, but do nothing to help it come to be.

Another example of sending a blessing: a wife blesses her husband with more patience and understanding in the name of Jesus, instead of sending him [by her thoughts] annoyance, disgust, anger, and worry. What fruit does this produce? She could have sent him a blessing in the name of Jesus: a blessing of peace, of a desire to change his life, to open his life to be a better person under the Lordship of Jesus Christ. This would have been a more constructive response which could have benefited her and her husband. In this way she would be cooperating with Jesus who is moving to help him to have a change of heart. St. Peter says, in 1Peter 3:9, when we bless we receive blessings in our life. Jesus Christ also taught us to give in order to receive: *"Give, and it will be given to you. A good measure, pressed down, shaken together, running over, will be put into your lap; for the measure you give will be the measure you get back."* (Luke 6: 38)

Many people believe praying for the person is a way to bless him/her. Undoubtedly, to pray for others is a blessing for them, but Jesus and St. Peter ask us explicitly also to bless, to send blessings. It is highly effective to bless a person in the name of Jesus and to proclaim it with faith-filled conviction, knowing the blessing, in cooperation with the grace of God which is already at work, will produce fruit. Then express your gratitude for what the Lord is doing and conclude with "amen," it is so, which signifies that we have done what Jesus asks of us.

Margarita: I see there is power in sending a blessing in Jesus' name, as well as the importance in asking the Lord to bless the person so he/she can be more fully what the Lord made the person to be.

Father: Right Margarita. It is also good to ask the Lord what blessing He would like you to extend in His name. He will probably show you more than what you seem to think the person needs.

The next two steps in the process of forgiveness are to receive more deeply what the Lord is doing with the offender or irritator and what He is doing within you, who have been offended or irritated.

5) VISUALIZE JESUS RISEN FROM THE DEAD, HAVING VICTORIOUSLY CONQUERED EVIL, TOUCHING BOTH OF YOU WITH HIS HEALING LOVE

Ask the Holy Spirit to give you an image of the offender without the defect being present due to the grace of God working with the forgiveness and blessing you have just proclaimed in the name of Jesus. Spend a little time enjoying the image of this forgiven and blessed person. Then pray:

Holy Father, this is [name of the person or the situation] **just the way I imagine him/her after having been forgiven and blessed by Jesus. Now, send Your Holy Spirit through me and make** [name of the person] **Your new creation, full of Your joy and Your peace.**

And for the hurt which has occurred within you, as you picture Jesus with His hands on your head, pray:

Heavenly Father, also heal my wounds created by this offense or irritation. I thank You because I know, through faith, You are healing me and attaining victory in me through Jesus Christ, Your Son, our

Lord. [Pause and take all the time you need so as to be conscious this is happening within you through the power of the Holy Spirit while thanking Him for this healing.]

Let the Holy Spirit bring about the transformation within you because you have the faith-filled conviction that the Lord is destroying the evil and bringing about new life.

Margarita, there are several ways to visualize the person transformed: 1) you can visualize the person like you remember the person, without the offense, 2) how you would think the person would be now without the offense and being blessed, or 3) you can ask the Lord to show you what the person would be like without this offense, but having been forgiven and blessed in Jesus' name. Hold on to that image. The Lord then gives you the new image of this transformed person replacing the image that was a life-depriving experience.

We are not inventing a new person, but rather we are expressing our faith that Jesus Christ is the Savior, destroying the evil and establishing the good. Therefore, He is transforming that person who has offended us because we have participated in His saving work by forgiving and blessing him/her in His name. It would be harmful to continue to imagine the person with the offense. It is, however, life-giving to hold onto the image of the person transformed through the power of the Cross of Jesus Christ convinced that Jesus is working with him/her outside you, while respecting his/her free-will.

As you visualize the transformation occurring as an expression of your faith in Jesus' saving power, you are participating in what He won on the Cross. It is because of your choice to forgive and bless this person in His name that Jesus is given permission to work within you and the offender more fully.

Margarita, it is my conviction that when I forgive someone, the Lord is present not only to transform the offender but also to heal me from the wrong or irritation. He comes to transform me in the deepest part of my being. I forgive the person not only with my mind, in recognizing the wrong, but also with my will, transferring the wrong to Jesus Christ crucified; and, He is helping me to accept this with my imagination; in other words I am forgiving using the imagination.

It has been my experience that often I forgive with my will, but I keep the image within me of the unforgiven person. It is very beneficial in the process of forgiving from the heart to receive in faith, through the grace of the Holy Spirit, the forgiven person within my imagination.

Before the forgiveness, the offender lives in two places: in the world and within me. It seems that when I forgive, the Lord gives me that person renewed within me. Thus he/she is present to give me life instead of taking it away. When I do this, I also participate more actively in Jesus' work of transforming the person in the world outside of me.

Even though I do not always see the transformation occurring outside of me, at least, I have the conviction, through faith, that Jesus is present healing me and is continuing to do the work that He was doing before I forgave the person. I am set free of this offence or irritation. How great and marvelous is the Lord, our Savior! There is no one like Him.

When I face the offender or I think about him, I find it important to give thanks to God that the person has been transformed within me. And I know by faith the process of transformation is occurring outside of me, even if my feelings do not immediately agree or if I do not instantly see the full transformation occurring.

Margarita: Father, this seems so powerful. However, the other person has free will. What if he/she do not choose to cooperate with this grace from the Lord, and instead rejects this new life Jesus wants to give him/her?

Father: Margarita, this is a good observation and a frequently asked question. This possibility does not worry me because I believe Jesus is the Savior, and He knows how to work with our free will. If it does not happen immediately for one reason or another, the Lord will triumph over evil, even if we do not see it. By faith He wants me to believe it. Then I leave this in the Lord's hands; He was sent not to condemn, but to save. My part is to forgive with the conviction that the wrong that I carried within is now in the hands of Christ Jesus, our Savior.

Before forgiving the person, I played the "role of the savior" toward this person by holding onto the offense. But after forgiving, I allow Jesus, instead of me, to be his/her Savior. My part now is to manifest more love toward this person. I will talk about it in greater detail in the last step.

Margarita: It is much better for Jesus to be the Savior of this person, instead of me usurping His place. I see now how my bad thoughts, words, and actions towards the offender did not help him/her, nor me.

Father, the wounds in my heart often do not leave quickly. As a matter of fact, sometimes it seems like they will never leave. I wonder what I should do when I continue to feel anger toward the person for all the wrong done to me.

Father: What you say is valid, Margarita. Many think that if that feeling remains, the offense or irritation is not forgiven, but this is not true. When we forgive in the name of Jesus, our Savior, it is done. We know this because of faith. For example: when, with a contrite heart, I ask the Lord to forgive my sins and with a firm purpose to take some steps to amend my life, by faith I know Jesus forgives me even if I do not feel like He did. This same faith is needed when I forgive another in the name of Jesus of Nazareth, our Savior; the Lord frees me from the offense. Then I allow Him to give me an image of the person forgiven and blessed by Him. This helps me to accept this new reality.

The problem, Margarita, is that sometimes we do not take time to be in the presence of the Lord for this process of forgiveness. We must ask and then take a few minutes to receive the healing for the irritation or offense. We are often impatient and want everything instantaneously.

At times it is also beneficial to have someone pray over us, so we can receive more deeply this victory. After doing this, still at times we may feel the irritation or the injustice. Again in this next step, I will discuss another key aspect of receiving forgiveness that often needs to be put into practice.

6) EXPRESS GRATITUDE AFTER THE PRAYER WE HAVE JUST SAID:

Keep thanking the Heavenly Father until you have a conviction of these changes occurring within you and also at work in the other person. If a new offense or irritation occurs, repeat the prayer in full from the beginning. This is in fulfillment of what Jesus said to Peter when Peter asked how often we should forgive another. Jesus said to forgive seventy times seven – always (Matthew 18: 22).

Margarita, when we give thanks to the Lord, we are proclaiming in faith His victory not only within ourselves, but also in the other person. Sometimes the irritations do not leave right away. But the act of receiving in faith through thanksgiving is a way of permitting the Lord to continue healing the wounds within you; this also allows us to participate with Him in doing an even deeper work of transformation in the offender.

In Agnes Sanford's book, Healing Light (pg. 53), she describes the act of receiving Jesus Christ's victory as follows:

"Having once accomplished forgiveness in His name, we must never question it, lest we stop the work that He is doing through us. Having said, 'I give thanks that so-and-so is forgiven,' we must keep on giving thanks that this is so. We must trust the actual working of God through us, and must not be misled by our own unruly feelings. The feeling toward the forgiven one may not immediately change. Indeed, the sense of revulsion and coldness that is the forerunner of death may be even more noticeable for a day or so. This is because we have dragged the half-forgotten dislike out over the threshold of consciousness, and like pulling up a tree by the roots it throws up a lot of dirt. Therefore, we need pay no attention to our feelings, knowing that they are only the result of an old thought habit of irritation and that they will soon pass away.

If a doctor removes a cinder from the eye, the discomfort may not go away immediately. The eye may feel worse for a few minutes, but that's all right. The doctor may say, 'your eye is still sore because it has been irritated for so long, but try to forget it.' So when the name or face of the person whom we have forgiven comes into mind again, perhaps with the usual irritation, we ought to think, 'That's nothing. Jesus Christ has forgiven so-and-so through me; therefore, she is forgiven, no matter how I feel. That feeling is only the old thought-habit, and it will soon go away'."

In a similar vein, I remember an experience when one of my cousins, who was a little over a year old, was crawling on the living room rug and all of a sudden started to scream in a real loud voice which was heard throughout the neighborhood. My uncle came into the living room and asked us who had dropped his little girl. We were all far from her. My aunt and uncle, convinced something had happened to her because she kept pointing to her knee while crying painfully, took her to the hospital. The x-ray results disclosed a needle had penetrated her knee without leaving a drop of blood. Administering anesthesia, the doctor removed the needle. Everybody returned home, without any major mishap. Nevertheless, after the anesthesia wore off, my cousin again began to scream as if the needle were still inside her knee. My aunt explained the needle had already been removed and the symptomatic 'ghost' pain she was sensing would disappear. Finally, after giving all the pertinent information, my aunt gave her the prescribed medicine for the pain, and my cousin was quiet while the affected area healed.

This is another example of how our emotions act when we are offended or irritated; the pain does not always go away immediately. We also may need time to heal once the offense and/or irritation is removed.

Margarita, after going through these steps of forgiveness with Jesus Christ, through the presence and power of the Holy Spirit, the cause of the wound, which is the hurt within you, is removed but the irritation sometimes stays a little longer. You must remind yourself that there is a healing process that is going on for this irritation. During this time, it is beneficial to maintain the forgiven person's image while thanking God for His victory within you. Agnes Sanford (p. 53) puts it this way, *"So when the name or face of the person whom we have forgiven comes into mind again, perhaps with the usual irritation, we ought to think, 'That's nothing. Jesus Christ has forgiven so-and-so through me, and therefore she is forgiven, no matter how I feel. That feeling is only the old thought-habit, and it will soon go away.'''*

It is also very beneficial to keep blessing the person, even as the irritation is diminishing. This will affirm the victory of Jesus over the effects of the offense while holding on to the transformed image of the offender. This is another way of affirming the conviction of your faith.

Sometimes you have to forgive seventy times seven times. If offended again by the same offender, keep forgiving with the same conviction. The Lord has His victory, so do not waver in believing this.

Jesus spoke about the importance of not wavering in our faith. In Mark 11:22-25 Jesus answered: *"'Have faith in God. Truly I tell you, if you say to this mountain, 'Be taken up and thrown into the sea,' and if you do not doubt in your heart, but believe that what you say will come to pass, it will be done for you. So I tell you, whatever you ask for in prayer, believe that you have received it, and it will be yours. Whenever you stand praying, forgive, if you have anything against anyone; so that your Father in heaven may also forgive you your trespasses."*

St. James in his letter also speaks of having faith without doubting. Even though he is speaking about asking for wisdom, we can apply this in regards to the process of forgiving others from the heart. In this process we also need unwavering faith: *"If any of you is lacking in wisdom* [or lacking the conviction in the steps of the process of forgiving others], *ask God, who gives to all generously and ungrudgingly, and it will be given you. But ask in faith, never doubting, for the one who doubts is like a wave of the sea, driven and tossed by the wind; for the doubter, being double-minded and unstable in every way, must not expect to receive anything from the Lord."* (James 1:5-8). James is emphasizing the importance of unwavering faith in order to receive what the Lord promises.

When you forgive and bless another, ask for the presence of the Holy Spirit to help you trust until you see the victory in yourself, as well as a conviction of what He is doing in the other person. Do not grow tired of asking for the presence of the Holy Spirit, with the powerful intercession of Mary, His beloved spouse, as a helper, throughout this entire process.

He wants us to have the victory Jesus Christ won through His cross and resurrection.

Margarita: Father, how do I know I have forgiven from the heart?

Father: You can be sure you have forgiven if , conscious of the powerful presence of the Holy Spirit with you, you: 1) truly have recognized the evil, 2) have proclaimed forgiveness and blessings in the name of Jesus; and 3) have visualized Jesus touching you and the other person and accepted the person transformed by Jesus in you, even if feelings of anger, irritation, disappointment, sadness or hurt still remain for a while. Continue to give thanks to God that you have done what He asked of you. It is not about forgetting or not ever thinking about the offense again, but it is about the fact that forgiveness is done. And you are accepting this without doubt. The wrong or irritation is on the cross of Jesus, and you have been freed from carrying it anymore.

There is a final step that is essential in the forgiveness process. This step is a fruit of the action of forgiving. But it is a vital next step after achieving the victory forgiveness produces.

7) EXPRESS LOVE TOWARDS THE PERSON OR SITUATION:

You can pray for this grace in the following prayer:

Heavenly Father, show me now what You want me to do so that I may express Your love in other ways toward the one who offended or irritated me, through some service or words, which could include words of correction when needed, yet with an attitude of love, with the conviction that Jesus is taking care of the offense and/or irritation.

In the world, the ones who do not believe in the victory of Jesus Christ think it is ridiculous to do good to overcome the evil others have done to us. Nevertheless our Teacher and Lord taught us the opposite: *"But I say to you that listen, Love your enemies, do good to those who hate you, bless those who curse you, pray for those who abuse you."* (Luke 6:27-28). And Romans 12:21 says: *"Do not be overcome by evil, but overcome evil with good."*

73

This is the time to pray for the person(s) and do other types of charitable things for them. It is incredible what love can accomplish. Let me tell you about the testimony of a woman I will call Sara. Sara had a boss who would mistreat and humiliate her every day. In spite of the mistreatment she decided to love her boss in words and deeds. With the strength of the Holy Spirit in prayer after having forgiven her, she decided to serve and to respect her boss in the way she spoke to her and the way she spoke about her in conversations with others. One day, her boss was so sick she had to be hospitalized and needed surgery. Sara sent her a letter expressing her genuine desire to see her get well and back at work. She also included a donation to help defray her expenses during her recuperation. Her boss was surprised to see how Sara was repaying her with charity and kindness even though she knew she had mistreated her. Upon her return, the boss changed towards Sara and they ended up developing a close friendship. Love in action won the victory.

Jesus Christ gave us some strong words in regards to this: *"In everything do to others as you would have them do to you."* (Matthew 7:12a). Imagine yourself doing to another person what you would like them to do to you, and then do it. Remember God is love and His love for us is eternal; it has no limits. He comes in order to empower us to love others in the same way.

Observe and listen to the words of Jesus in John 13:12-15: *"After he had washed their feet, had put on his robe, and had returned to the table, he said to them, 'Do you know what I have done to you? You call me Teacher and Lord--and you are right, for that is what I am. So if I, your Lord and Teacher, have washed your feet you also ought to wash one another's feet. For I have set you an example, that you also should do as I have done to you."*

Jesus wants to make sure His message is clear when He says to His disciples, *"I give you a new commandment, that you love one another. Just as I have loved you, you also should love one another. By this everyone will know that you are my disciples, if you have love for one another."* (John 13: 34-35).

Another act of love we can do is to ask forgiveness from the one who has offended us, for the way we responded incorrectly, in words or actions, to their offense. For example, if someone says something unjust or incorrect and our response is anger with hurtful words, we will need to love this person by asking for forgiveness for reacting in this way. This act of humility creates the opportunity for the person who has offended us to repent also for the way they have mistreated us. This is how reconciliation can be accomplished.

It is vital to mention that our acts of love should not encourage the vice in the offender as, for example, giving a bottle of wine to an alcoholic, but should be acts of love that can benefit without enabling a person in their vice(s).

Another helpful point that I have found very important when someone has offended and/or irritated me is to ask the Lord: "Lord, have I previously experienced a similar offense and/or irritation, or a similar response to this current offense/irritation, in my lifetime including in my childhood?" If the Lord brings someone or situation to mind, I need to forgive that person and/or situation so as to remove a root cause of my current irritation. What freedom and newness of life this forgiving from the heart brings!

Margarita: I think I wanted forgiveness to be something simple. I used to say something like: "well the offense has been done; what can I do about it now? I'll just try to forget it. I am going to go on living as if it never happened." I wanted forgiveness to be something that would not take time or any special effort. But now I see that if an offense or irritation comes especially from a person close to me, I need to take more time to go through all seven steps of forgiving and blessing so as to receive in the name of Jesus Christ new life for that person and myself.

I can see how this process will benefit me by giving me freedom and peace while helping the other person.

Father: I want to explain something else that can make the whole process even more enriching. It has to do with the merciful presence of our Father giving us Jesus, in His Spirit, through the Sacraments. The Sacraments, which Jesus established, will help you obtain an even more complete victory over the evil effects that frustrations and offenses of other people can create.

CHAPTER 6

The Power of Encountering Jesus through the Sacraments

[Especially through the Sacraments of Reconciliation and the Eucharist]

Father: Margarita, before finishing the subject of forgiving others, I would like to explain the importance of the sacraments to obtain the victory over any frustrations other people may cause in us.

Margarita: Father, please explain what the word 'sacrament' means and why they are important in my life with Jesus, in His Body, the Church, and in the process of forgiving from the heart.

Father: A sacrament is not a "thing" but an encounter with Christ Jesus Who died and rose to give us abundance of life. The word "Sacrament" means a sensible sign established by Jesus through which He, in the action of the Holy Spirit, is present to transmit grace, His special help, to us. Jesus Christ Himself established these sacraments to continue His presence and saving work in the midst of His Body, the Church, after His ascension into heaven.

In the Catechism of the Catholic Church (CCC)# 1146 we read: *"In human life, signs and symbols occupy an important place. As a being at once body and spirit, man expresses and perceives spiritual realities through physical signs and symbols. As a social being, man needs signs and symbols to communicate with others through language, gestures, and actions. The same holds true for his relationship with God."*

Here is an example to help you understand this. There was a woman who was blind and deaf. Was it impossible to communicate with her? One would think so. But she had a mind and will which she wished to use in order to communicate with others. The people around her, likewise, had their own thoughts which they desired to communicate to her. Was it possible? Yes, it was possible through another sense, the faculty of touch. This woman was Helen Keller. She and the people in her environment learned to communicate through touch.

We, as human beings, need to be in communication with other people including God. This communication is obtained through sensible signs using any one or several of the five senses; otherwise communication is not possible. When Jesus Christ was among us, He was the Heavenly Father's sacrament, in a broad sense, a sensible sign of the Father communicating with us in a human way to impart special graces to us. Now, after His resurrection, He is alive and present to us in the sacraments. Therefore, He established these sacraments to continue His communication with us in a human way, the communication of His presence and His transforming grace for us. The sacraments are sensible signs through which He is in a personal contact with us and gives us His special graces.

This is explained in the Catechism of the Catholic Church.

1116 *"Sacraments are 'powers that come forth' from the Body of Christ (Luke 5:17, 6:19, 8:46) which is ever-living and life-giving. They are actions of the Holy Spirit at work in his Body, the Church. They are the masterworks of God in the new and everlasting covenant."*

1123 *"The purpose of the sacraments is to sanctify men, build up the Body of Christ and to give worship to God. Because they are signs they also instruct, they not only presuppose faith, but by words and objects they also nourish, strengthen, and express it. That is why they are called 'sacraments of faith (SC 59)."*

1129 *"The Church affirms that, for believers, the sacraments of the New Covenant are necessary for salvation (cf Cc. of Trent: DS 1604). 'Sacramental grace' is the grace of the Holy Spirit, given by Christ and proper to each sacrament. The Spirit heals and transforms those who receive him by conforming them to the Son of God. The fruit of the sacramental life is that the Spirit of adoption makes the faithful partakers*

in the divine nature (cf 2 Peter 1:4) by uniting them in a living union with the only Son, the Savior."

This explanation does not contain all the depth of a sacrament, but it can help you understand a little more what the sacraments are.

As we consider forgiving others: in the Sacrament of Reconciliation or Confession, Jesus is present to give us His grace and His strength as we confess our sins with contrite hearts, including when we failed to forgive others who offended us.

In other words, in the process of forgiving others we need to confess the improper way we have handled these offenses or irritations. When we humble ourselves and acknowledge these sins and repent, Jesus extends His forgiveness in a human encounter through the words of absolution proclaimed by the bishop or the priest. In addition, He gives us His grace to experience a life free from the offense. He also helps us more easily and fully in future difficult moments to react in a more life giving way, namely, to forgive others more immediately when feeling upset by an offense or an apparent offense. Also in this Sacrament, as we leave these wrongs of others in His hands, He liberates us from the evil effects that we experienced. In this way, the Sacrament of Reconciliation is extremely helpful in the process of forgiving another from the heart.

In the Sacrament of the Holy Eucharist, Jesus is present to continue to feed what He initiates in the Sacrament of Reconciliation. In the Sacrament of Reconciliation, in faith we surrender from the heart the evil which we have done, such as holding resentment against the person or expressed anger to the person who offended us. Jesus forgives us and assures us of His victory over the evil in us as well as in the other person. Now in the Sacrament of the Eucharist or Communion, in the physical presence of Jesus, we let the Lord nourish us and heal us from the hurt done to us. He also strengthens us to forgive more immediately in future situations. He also strengthens the image of the transformed person whom we have forgiven. Thus in the Eucharist, Jesus is completing His work of healing our hearts of the evil we experienced. At the same time, He assures us He is realizing the transformation of our offender.

Jesus Christ intends through these Sacraments, with word and action, to continue His mission of liberating His people from evil while giving them His life in abundance.

All of this requires faith in what Jesus Christ established within His Church. They also move us to a faith in His work of restoring us in our covenant relationship with Himself and His people.

The Sacrament of Reconciliation is also a useful moment of encounter with Jesus so as to confess our improper response to God for what has been termed "forgiving God" (chapter 1) for evils that we or others have done. The Lord then is really present to heal the way we have improperly responded while giving us a greater strength in future situations to respond more correctly. In the Eucharist, Jesus is present to continue this transforming work and to develop an ever more profound union with Himself. In this union we have a clearer understanding of God and His activity in the different situations of our lives.

Margarita: Father, so the Sacraments are real encounters with the living Jesus who is present in them. In the Sacrament of Reconciliation I can repent, and He frees me. He is present through His Spirit to continue the process of restoring what evil has done within me. In the Eucharist, He is also present. So when I receive Communion, He empowers me with special strength to receive an ever deeper healing of the wounds which I experienced.

Father: That's it, Margarita! We need both the Sacrament of Reconciliation and the Eucharist. We also need to spend time after receiving them to be aware of what each of these sacramental encounters with Jesus is doing. In the Sacrament of Reconciliation, Jesus is freeing us from our sins and those of the offender. He also gives us His grace and His strength to react in a more life-giving way.

In the Eucharist, it is good to bring all you have been doing in the process of forgiving another, so He can purify this through His sacrifice. Then we receive more deeply His healing presence. He is also available to help us with wisdom, to direct us and empower us to show His love for the offender.

Margarita: Father, I see more clearly now, how these Sacraments can be immensely helpful in having a living encounter with Jesus. This encounter assists me in forgiving from the heart the offenses and even the irritations of others.

CHAPTER 7
Testimonies

Father: There are many testimonies, Margarita, I can share from the implementation of this process of forgiveness. Here are just a few:

1) A lady, whom I will call Rosa [some details are altered so as not to be able to identify this person], came with a big burden of having been oppressed at her job by her boss for the last fifteen years. He mistreated her in that he was very demanding. He would ask her to do more than would be reasonable for the type of work she was doing. He did not pay her a just wage. After listening to her story which was filled with years of suffering with her boss, I suggested she look for a job elsewhere. She told me she lacked the training to go to another job. Rosa could not even consider moving to another city because her husband had a good job and they, with their children, had lived in their current home for twenty years. The work she was doing was something she was especially trained to do, and she also enjoyed it. The constant badgering from her boss is what made her life miserable.

I suggested she try implementing the process of forgiveness from the heart. This, I told her would at least help her find some inner peace by knowing that the whole situation was in our Lord's hands. He would heal the inner hurts, and she could also participate with Jesus in working more fully with her boss having begun this process within herself. I explained how Jesus, when allowed to be the Savior over all that was happening, could lead her to His peace while He would continue His work for her boss' transformation. She agreed, somewhat reluctantly, to take the steps of forgiveness. Rosa kept telling me she felt it would be difficult to believe that a change was possible. I reminded her that this belief would be judging and condemning him, and her disbelief was also implying that God had no power to transform the heart of her boss. I asked her again to ask the

Holy Spirit to help her believe in this transformation which seemed so impossible to her.

Rosa returned after a week and said she was feeling more at peace even though her boss did not seem to be changing. I asked her to do the first three steps, in the forgiveness process, first thing each morning. Then when he called she could be doing the last four steps interiorly while listening to him speak to her on the phone. In order to do this, I explained, it would be helpful to have the prayer by the phone so that when he called, instead of responding in an angry and frustrating way, she could listen to him while praying interiorly these last four steps of the forgiveness process.

After a few weeks of doing this, she came to see me with great joy. I asked her how things were going. She said she could not believe the transformation that happened. Rosa explained that her boss called one day as was his custom. But this time he was different; he apologized for all the times he had mistreated her and promised to give her a salary increase which her line of work merited. It was more than what she expected. Since then, he has continued to treat her with more respect.

Rosa said that although she understood all I shared with her about forgiveness, she had some doubts it would really produce any real effect. Nevertheless she started the process of forgiving and the blessing in the name of Jesus accompanied with the visualization. She imagined this person without his defects and seeing him the way she thought he would be once forgiven and blessed. Then she became more peaceful within herself thanks to the healing presence of Jesus. She was most surprised when she experienced him changed.

She told me that from this experience, she was planning on developing this process as a way of life for all offensive and/or annoying situations. In her situation I saw how mighty our God is in bringing about His victory in our hearts and even reaching out to the offender.

It was so good to hear Rosa's testimony, Margarita. It helped me too. I know I have experienced greater freedom within myself even if the other person who offended me did not change as dramatically as her boss did. I have a deeper conviction that practicing these steps will produce a great effect in me and in the other person in a very profound way.

2) I remember a young man years ago. I will call him Luke. Luke was about 23 years old and dying of cancer; the doctors did not give him much hope. During this time there was a missionary who was working with me and the other priests in the parish. Since the house of this young man was nearby, I asked this lady, the missionary, to visit and pray with him as often as possible. In her visits she uncovered hurts from his past that he needed to forgive. This man forgave and blessed in the name of Jesus several people and situations in his life. The young man, because he forgave, began to feel more inner peace. Within several weeks, the doctor told him that he was totally healed of the cancer. He forgave and blessed in the name of Jesus Christ the people in his past who had offended or irritated him. Then he took time to imagine these offenders being touched by Jesus without their defects, but as he thought they should have been. This allowed Jesus not only to give him more inner peace but also to heal him of cancer.

Margarita, my question is: Could some illnesses exist today for lack of 'forgiveness and blessing'? Through the grace of the Jesus' death and resurrection forgiveness heals the offended one and can even bring about physical healing as happened with Luke. I have seen people healed of physical ailments as soon as they forgave in the process I have explained to you. I also have heard of cases that this forgiveness brings newness of life in some way to the ones who had done the wrongs.

3) Margarita, I want to present now two testimonies from Agnes Sanford's book, *Healing Light*. She describes what happened after implementing forgiveness and blessing in the name of Jesus while visualizing the others without the defect.

I learned this method by experimenting with my own children. When one of them came in cross and unhappy, instead of flying into a temper, I would quiet myself and by faith make in my mind the picture of the child as he was at his best [having been forgiven and blessed]. *'Heavenly Father, that's your little child as you want him to be,' I would say. 'Please send Your Holy Spirit through me now and make him be that way, happy and peaceful and kind. Thank You, because I believe You are doing so. Amen.'* I would *then hold firmly to the picture of the bright-faced, happy child whom I wanted to see. And in less than a minute, the child would change and the thing that I had seen in my mind would be brought forth.*

We are indeed made in His image and likeness. He is first of all Creator-and so are we. (in the sense of participating in God's work of re-creating or transforming what He has made). *The more we practice the work of creation the more easily and naturally His power works through us. After a few months of practice, I found that my prayers could influence my children by 'remote control,' as my daughter expressed it. If I heard angry voices anywhere in the house, I had only to make in my mind the image of a child at peace and project it into reality by the word of faith. And after a time, this work was accomplished and there was no more need to think about it, for my children lived in peace together from day's beginning to day's end.*

'Blessed are the peacemakers' said the Teacher.

The creation of peace in someone else, by projecting into that one the love of God, is true forgiveness, remission of sins, the changing of the other person, so that the quality in him that has annoyed us will not be there anymore. If we really try forgiveness we find out for ourselves that this is so, for people sometimes change before us in a most amazing way." (Pp. 54-55)

What she is saying is the following: when we forgive and bless in the name of Jesus while holding this person transformed within our imagination, we will be surprised by the results within us and in the offender.

4) Margarita, here is the other testimony from Healing Light: *"I once outlined to an intelligent and open-minded mother this method of changing someone through God's love.*

'What can I do about my little girl?' The mother asked. 'She is the strangest child she never smiles! She worries and worries because she thinks she isn't pretty and people don't like her. She isn't very pretty, really; she's so scrawny and thin. But she'd look prettier if she smiled...And the worst thing is she doesn't seem to have any affection for me or anyone else. She

thinks I don't love her. Of course I do, but she does make me cross! What can I do?'

Stand beside her when she's asleep and lay your hands on her, as you no doubt found out when she was a tiny baby, and you could soothe her with your hands. Then say to yourself, 'By faith I see my child loving and happy and openhearted and well, as God made her and wants her to be. And in the name of Jesus Christ, I say that this shall be'....

'But I am not a Christian,' the mother stated with admirable frankness'

'Then try it anyway,' I said, hoping that as she worked in harmony with God, who is love, God would help her whether she knew Him or not. 'Make the picture of the child as you want her to be, and say, 'My love brought this child into the world, and through my own mother-love I re-create her after this image. And I left in some trepidation.

A month later I saw this lady at a meeting of the PTA. 'It worked,' she beamed. 'I never saw anything like it in my life! The next morning Susie came to my bedside and smiled, and said, 'Good morning, Mother,' and kissed me! And she's been like a different child ever since! She's happy, and she's gained weight and she's much prettier.

I need not have wondered whether it would work. God is always much more broad-minded than I am. Two years have passed. The results of this prayer experiment have continued to grow, and both mother and daughter are now Christians.

There is no more joyful thing in the entire world than an act of love that sets free the forgiveness of Christ in another. The first step in forgiveness is overcoming resentment; that is, learning to like someone whom one has not liked before. The second step, which should follow spontaneously and naturally upon the first, is the re-creation of the forgiven one by love. Having forgiven someone, we do not see his faults any more. Instead of that, we see his virtues, creating in our minds by faith the exact opposite of the traits that had annoyed us in him, and projecting them by faith into reality. These good and happy traits will often rise to the surface and be manifest, as if they had been there all the time only awaiting the touch of love to bring them forth. This does not always happen, of course. Some people's minds are closed so tight that love seems to beat against them in vain. But even in cases like this, love may plant a seed in the mind of the forgiven one and that seed may bring forth fruit sometime, somewhere.

The one who prays thus is like a gardener. When he pours out upon his fellowman the forgiveness of God he often sees that man comes to life as a parched plant comes to life when water is poured upon it. And seeing this, his faith is increased. For the sake of our own joy and faith, then, let us practice sending forth the forgiving love of God not only toward those whom we have learned to like, not only toward our irritating children and to the problem people around us, but also toward any person whom we see in need. If we try this as a solemn duty, it may not work. Prayer needs wings of joy to fly upon. But if we do it happily and spontaneously, as a sort of game, we will often see it work right before our eyes." (Pp. 55-57).

5) Margarita, Josyp Terelya in his book *The Witness* shared this testimony. Josyp was imprisoned in Siberia because of his faith in Christ. He was dying from the freezing cold weather inside his cell. He suffered overwhelmingly from hypothermia. It was in this situation that the Blessed Mother, the Virgin Mary, appeared to him. He thought she would cover him with her mantle, but instead, she asked him to forgive his enemies. Her request was the last thing he could have imagined. All he was worried about was how to keep his body warm; nevertheless, she said to forgive so God's grace could be made manifest in him. He complied with her request; he forgave his enemies and those who had unjustly imprisoned him. Josyp felt warmth.

When the guards came to check on him, they were surprised as they saw he had taken off the only clothing he had left: a T-shirt. They called the doctors who were expecting to find him dead from hypothermia. When they saw him they asked him if he was practicing some type of yoga. He told them the Virgin Mary had appeared and had invited him to forgive his enemies. Mary, our mother, also wants us to forgive those who offend us so that her Son may liberate us and heal us. Mary's intercession is powerful in this process of forgiving others.

Margarita: Thank you again, Father. I now know the tremendous importance and power of forgiveness. I know more fully what it is to forgive from the heart. What you have taught me I plan to practice every day of my life. I will use this powerful tool with God's grace. I will no longer need to carry the burden of others' offenses or irritations. Through forgiveness I can now live with a new freedom and the newness of life that Jesus offers me.

CHAPTER 8
Indicators When to Forgive

Margarita: One more thing Father, can we review some more indicators that would tell me when I need to forgive?

You gave me some already, such as feelings of irritation or annoyance from what someone said or did. Or when someone has offended me, even though I do not feel anger, I need to forgive. And obviously, if I am angry or hold resentment against someone, this too needs my forgiveness. You also said if I sinned along with another person, I need to forgive that person even if I have already repented of my part, my sin. Are there other ways to be conscious of the need to forgive?

Father: I am going to give you, Margarita, a list you can use as a guide including some of the indicators that you already mentioned. I hope you find it helpful in recognizing some of the times when forgiveness is needed.

I FEEL:

- Anger

- Hatred

- Rage

- Resentment

- Revenge

- Disgust

- Frustration

- Irritation

- Anxiety

- Discouragement

- Sadness about what someone has said or done or some situation

- A sense of worthlessness because of what another has said to me

- Hurt

TOWARD:

- Person(s)

- Situation(s)

WHEN I AM:

- Criticizing

- Gossiping

- Complaining (even interiorly)

- Judging

- Condemning

WHEN:

- Someone has participated in my sin.

- I think that someone has something against me.

- I think that he/she does not like me or is even wishing me something evil

- I want to see things change in another [ex. that a family member have a more living faith-life].

- I have been insulted or abused.

- I have parents who have not loved each other.

- I have parents who were absent (not there very often or not at all).

- I have parents who divorced or separated.

- I know someone who is distant from the Lord and needs to return to Him.

Margarita, this chart will give you some examples of when there is a need to forgive. I think I have explained most of these. Forgiveness will set you free and enable you to participate with Jesus in bringing His mercy even more fully to that person, the offender.

There are some cases, however, where individuals suspect that others dislike them for some reason. Even when there are suspicions that another dislikes you, forgiveness frees you and allows God to work in that person.

I have also met individuals who have told me they believe someone has placed a curse on them. Forgiving the person enables God to free you from the anxiety or worry as He breaks the evil from the person. By forgiving and blessing in the name of Jesus, I participate in the Lord breaking the evil in and from that person. I am then working with Jesus, who in His mercy, is enabling him/her to change from being an instrument of evil to being an instrument of life and happiness.

I also know of some people who suspect somebody is planning to do something unjust, or something evil. Forgiveness again frees the person who has anxiety about this and allows Jesus to work more fully in transforming that person(s).

Another situation in need of forgiveness is when a person is irritated, but there is no one at fault. For example, when I was a small child, fourteen months old, my mother had to go to the hospital to give birth to my brother. I was told that I was terribly upset and cried uncontrollably during the time she was away, except when I slept, probably from exhaustion. She was not at fault, nor was I. I was only a baby. She was only doing what was needed in her situation. However, I reacted in a way that manifested strong disappointment or anger. I received greater peace and inner freedom after I forgave my mother for what had happened. What I was forgiving was the situation with my perception as a baby as to what I thought was my mother's fault. After doing this I had a whole new way of perceiving her. I also responded in a better way to my mother.

Many people have told me about their concerns for their sons, daughters or other family members who have apparently left God out of their lives as well as everything that has to do with Him. These and similar situations are also indicators that the process of forgiveness from the heart is needed.

Another comment: if I criticize a situation or person, I have another indicator that I need to forgive from the heart that situation or person. When I criticize I am revealing a frustration, a disappointment that I have and which I am holding within myself. It comes out in the form of the criticism.

Another time to remember to forgive from the heart is when you get upset about a situation where no person is involved, for example, having a flat tire on the way to work. This is an occasion where, forgiving what is happening enables one to handle this situation with greater peace.

In these moments as in the above I have found that the Lord is calling me to forgive and to allow Him to work in the situation in order to free me of anxiety, disappointment, anger, etc ... while He works His good both for me and the other person.

Often some people say, "but so and so does not deserve forgiveness." I think the Lord might say: "that might be true, but as you forgive you can be free of their broken condition. You need to let Me be the Savior, and not yourself, over what is going on." If you think He wants you to say or do something after you have forgiven them, then you need to do what He is asking and trust that He is working in the situation.

It is also helpful to remember for those whom we think did not deserve to be forgiven, that we ourselves do not deserve to be forgiven for our sins. But the Lord in His mercy has forgiven us. Then He calls us to be merciful as He has been with us.

Margarita: This really helps. I now realize how important forgiveness is and how free and more alive I could be if I forgive from the heart, in the name of Jesus. I want Him to be my Savior. I see now I have been trying to make myself the savior in my different situations, instead of Jesus. I want to learn to surrender all my hurts and upsetting situations to Jesus, so I can have a greater abundance of life and experience His victory in me and through me to another.

I also see I need to keep thanking Jesus after I have forgiven. By doing this I am expressing my faith (believing) that He is healing the evil effect within me and working in the other people that I am forgiving even when I do not immediately feel or see this. I certainly need His grace to believe this. I have such a tendency to let my feelings move me to believe that nothing is happening or that I cannot be free of the irritation I have.

Father: Margarita, now you understand better the power of forgiving and blessing in the name of Jesus Christ. This comes forth once forgiveness from the heart is practiced towards offensive or irritating persons (and situations).

Now having studied the seven step process in order to forgive from the heart, I present the entire process as a prayer form. Knowing better what forgiveness is, I pray this prayer will help you to allow the healing and vivifying power of "forgiveness from the heart" to impact your life, filling you and others, with the freedom and abundance of life which Jesus comes to offer us.

CHAPTER 9

The Whole Process Summarized in a Prayer

To forgive, in a few words, is, in communion with the powerful action of the Holy Spirit: , 1) to be conscious of an offense and/or irritation, while 2) surrendering it to Jesus Christ on His cross and then 3) receiving through faith His victory for both you, the offended person, and for the offender(s) followed by acts of genuine loving responses to the offender.

Thus to realize these three aspects, there are seven steps to follow in order to help one forgive from the heart. Praying all seven steps and taking time alone with the Lord is especially valuable when the offense or irritation is more profound or serious. For less serious offenses steps one, four, and five, may be sufficient.

HERE IS THE WHOLE PROCESS OF FORGIVING FROM THE HEART SUMMARIZED IN A PRAYER

Preparation to forgive from the heart:

1. Ask for the presence of the Holy Spirit:

God, my Father, fill me with Your Holy Spirit so I can forgive from the heart. I receive Your Holy Spirit by imagining His presence as if He were a light that fills a dark room. Thank You, Heavenly Father, for empowering me with His presence to be my guide and support. [Spend a little time being conscious of receiving this presence of the Holy Spirit.]

2. Become conscious of the reality of God's love towards you and towards

the others who have offended or irritated you:

God, my Father, You are wonderful. You sent Your Son, Jesus Christ to show us Your mercy. I praise You for Your love. You manifested this love by sending us Your Son as man, in order to have Him live as one of us, to teach us, to die for our sins, to rise to give us a new life, and to send us Your Holy Spirit. Help me to be conscious of this love. [Then in the silence of your heart take an image of His love to gaze upon, such as a crucifix, and then listen to the Lord say your name while you read a biblical text of God's love for you, such as John 15:13: ...(Your name) *"No one has greater love than this, to lay down one's life for one's friends."* Or Jeremiah 31:3, "... (Your name) *I have loved you with an everlasting love; therefore I have continued my faithfulness to you."* Stop here and take time to receive this until the phrase resounds deeply within you and then thank the Lord for this love.]

I thank You, Lord, for Your loving presence which helps me forgive the offenses and/or irritations of [name the person(s) or situation(s)]. **I thank You because You want to save every one of us from all sin and all its evil effects.**

3. Receive God's mercy for you:

Heavenly Father, help me to see my sins and to remember the mercy You have shown me.

[Take a few minutes to remember your past sins and the many times He has forgiven you so as to thank Him for His forgiveness and mercy. If there is a sin for which you have not yet been forgiven, seek His forgiving love at this time, especially for having held onto the offense or irritation of another or responded incorrectly towards them or in any way you too have sinned in a similar way as the offender(s). We need to be honest before the Lord while seeking His mercy for sins we have committed. Take advantage of this moment after being aware of your own sins to pray.]

Jesus, please forgive me and wash me with Your Precious Blood, which

You shed to save me from all sin and from the tendency to repeat these evils.

[Take enough time so as to have an interior conviction of this grace of His forgiveness towards you. Imagine yourself filled with the purifying light of His mercy. Sense yourself in this presence and allow the Lord to touch your heart with His forgiveness, His mercy. Remember the importance and victory that comes as you confess your sins through the encounter with Jesus in the Sacrament of Reconciliation. Utilize this Sacrament in this process of forgiving from the heart.]

THE ACTUAL PRAYER OF FORGIVENESS FROM THE HEART

4. Forgive and bless in the name of Jesus:

[Imagine yourself with Jesus crucified on Calvary and with Mary, His mother, at your side. This is where sin, death, and the kingdom of darkness were conquered.

It is best to express God's mercy for one person or situation at a time unless several people are involved in the same offense.]

Heavenly Father, surround this person or situation with the light of Your presence and love. And Father, I thank You for Your infinite mercy for him/her.

[Then visualize the person(s) surrounded with the light of Christ and say:]

With the power of the Holy Spirit and in the name of our Lord Jesus Christ crucified, I forgive you for [take time to mention the offense or fault bringing to mind when it actually happened and be conscious of any feelings that may have been present.] **And I give thanks that you are now forgiven through Jesus. Amen.**

And in the name of our Lord Jesus Christ crucified, I bless you with [mention the particular thing that you think this person or situation needed in order to be better.] **And I give thanks because you are now being**

blessed. Amen. [To proclaim that it is being done and saying "Amen" affirms that I have completed what Jesus asks of me. I am also expressing my faith that He is continuing His work of salvation in me, the offended one, and is working His grace of salvation within the offender.]

5. [Receive the forgiveness by visualizing Jesus, with His wounds but now risen and victorious over all evils, touching both of you with His healing love:

Ask the Holy Spirit to give you an image of the offender without the presence of the defect. Spend time visualizing this forgiven and blessed person(s). Then pray]

God, our Heavenly Father, this is [name the person or the situation] **just the way I imagine him/her after having been forgiven and blessed by Jesus. Now, send Your Holy Spirit through me and make** [name the person] **Your new creation, full of Your joy and Your peace.**

Heavenly Father, also heal the wounds within me caused by this offense or irritation. I thank You because I know, through faith, that You are healing me and are realizing a victory in me through Jesus Christ, Your Son, our Lord.

[Take all the time you need so as to be conscious of this happening through the power of the cross of Jesus while thanking Him for this healing of your emotional reaction interiorly or exteriorly.]

6. Receive the victory by expressing thanks after the prayer:

[Keep thanking the Father until you notice, or at least have a conviction, of the change occurring in you and the other person. If a new offense or irritation happens, repeat the entire prayer.]

7. Express more love toward the person or situation:

Most loving Father, show me now what You want me to do, so as to express Your love in various other ways toward the one who has offended and/or irritated me, through some service and/or words, including words of correction, if so needed, but with a loving attitude of kindness coming from my having forgiven and blessed him/her from the heart in Your name and knowing You are destroying the evil and establishing Your victory through grace. Thank You. Amen.

Conclusion

Sensing what Jesus wants of you and with His grace, practice forgiving the offenses and/or irritations of others <u>daily</u>. This practice will give you a greater inner peace and harmony because in the process of forgiveness the offensive person is transformed first and foremost within you. This also enables the Lord to use you in helping the person outside of you to become a better person.

Therefore, it is best after forgiving to continue blessing the person with what you sensed, when they offended you, was needed so as to be a better person while thanking the Lord for His saving work that He is doing within them. Also continue showing love in thoughts, words, and/or deeds, as the person outside of you becomes a person responding more faithfully to the Lord.

My blessing: May the understanding and daily usage of this process of forgiveness bring you the peace of God *"Keep on doing the things that you have learned and received and heard and seen in me, and the God of peace will be with you."* - Phil. 4:9. And with God's favor and through the merits of Jesus Christ's death and resurrection and by means of the presence and the power of the Holy Spirit, may you now be experiencing more joy and peace in place of burdens and frustration or even depression. May the Heavenly Father through Jesus Christ, His Son and our Lord, and in the Holy Spirit bless you abundantly + in the name of the Father, and of the Son and of the Holy Spirit and give you His peace! And may Mary, our most merciful Mother, continue accompanying and praying for you in order to live more fully in the victory of Christ Jesus. Amen.

Fr. Francis A. Frankovich, CC

About the Author

Fr. Frankovich was born in Barstow, California in 1942 to Eleanor and Albert Frankovich. He is the elder of two sons. He entered St. Francis De Sales Seminary in 1960 which was located on the campus of the University of San Diego. On the same campus from Immaculate Heart Seminary he was ordained a priest May 31, 1968 for the Diocese of San Diego, California. He served 10 years in various parishes in the San Diego Diocese and then, when the Diocese of San Diego was split forming two dioceses, he served 11years in the Diocese of San Bernardino which included two years serving in the Diocesan Serra House of Formation for Seminarians in Riverside. During his years as a priest he studied for a Master's Degree in Theology at the Franciscan University of Steubenville, Ohio. He also attended Creighton University in Omaha, Nebraska for a certificate in Spiritual Direction while assisting the Institute for Priestly Formation (IPF) on that campus.

With the permission of his bishop in 1989, he went to join the Companions of the Cross. As a Companion, he served at St. Mary's in Ottawa, Canada as their Pastor and then spent three years working in the formation of seminarians before being assigned to be the Director of the Catholic Charismatic Center (CCC) in Houston, Texas. After six years as Director, he was assigned to continue at the CCC working with the Spanish-speaking community in areas of evangelization and formation where he continues to minister.

Fr. Francis has been invited and has participated in evangelistic events in Mexico, Colombia, El Salvador, Honduras, Panama, Peru, and in the Dominican Republic. On one of his visits to Colombia, he was asked to write a book. After prayerful consideration, he sensed that he was to write about forgiveness. Working through this issue in his own life and seeing the tremendous need to understand and practice forgiveness in a way that

105

is practical and produces fruit, he wrote this book in Spanish. After several revisions, the current book *Perdonando de Corazón* and its counterpart in English *Forgiving from the Heart* have been published.

May this small book be a source of direction for a path to greater freedom and abundance of life found in Christ Jesus!

Connect with the Companions of the Cross online!

companionscross.org | Discover the spirituality, brotherhood and mission of the Companions of the Cross and how you can participate

vocations.companionscross.org | Explore a vocation to the priesthood with the Companions of the Cross

Like us on Facebook

COMPANIONS OF THE CROSS:
facebook.com/companionsofthecross

Follow us on Twitter

COMPANIONS OF THE CROSS:
twitter.com/CompanionsCross

Subscribe to our YouTube channel

youtube.com/user/CompanionsCross

Companions of the Cross

We are a Roman Catholic community of priests, committed
to living and ministering together as brothers in the Lord.
God has called us to labour boldly for the renewal of the Church through a dynamic
evangelization centered upon Christ crucified, who is God's power and wisdom.
Spurred on by the love of God, we desire all people to come into the fullness of life
through a personal and ongoing encounter with Jesus Christ.

Spirituality
LOVE FOR CHRIST CRUCIFIED, A SPIRITUALITY OF GOD'S
POWER AND WISDOM | Jesus's death on the cross and resurrection saved the
world. Therefore, we fully commit ourselves
to him; seek his will in all we do; and trust in his power to do it.

We Are:
- Men of the Eucharist
- Led and empowered by the Holy Spirit
- Truly devoted to Mary
- Loyal to the Magisterium

Brotherhood
LOVE FOR ONE ANOTHER, A LIFE OF TRUE BROTHERHOOD
We base ourselves on the model of Jesus and his disciples, who lived together,
ministered together, and supported one another.

Mission
LOVE FOR THE CHURCH, A MISSION OF EVANGELIZATION
AND RENEWAL | We invite all people into an initial and ongoing encounter with
Jesus. As we are transformed by his love, we bring about authentic renewal in the
Church and world.

 Companions of the Cross

199 Bayswater Avenue, Ottawa, ON Canada K1Y 2G5 | 1.866.885.8824
1949 Cullen Blvd, Houston, TX USA 77087-3553 | 1.866.724.6073
WWW.COMPANIONSCROSS.ORG

- Bloom who you are
  Retreat in
    Florida

Philippians 4 -
VI - Instructions for
     the community

4 - Joy & Peace

Rejoice in the Lord always. I shall
say it again, rejoice.
5. Your kindness should be known
   to all. the Lord is near -

6. Have no anxiety at all,
   but in everything, by prayer
and petition, with thanksgiving
                   make your requests
                   known to God -